The Taco Cookbook

100 Favorite Taco Recipes From The Flavorful Mexican Kitchen

TAN ACERO

ISBN-13: 978-1545156537

ISBN-10: 1545156530

DEDICATION

To those who love good food

TABLE OF CONTENTS

INTRODUCTION

Among Mexican street foods, Tacos is the most popular, and the first to have crossed the border into the United States. Even at that, it still maintained its popularity to such an extent that Korean cuisines are finding out how they can use them to sell their own indigenous dishes. A few other expensive restaurants that specialize in cultural dishes have also begun to include tacos on their menus.

As a matter of fact, the last few decades have brought about an explosive increase of Mexican foods into the United States. Taco trucks are everywhere! Packaged tortillas and tortilla chips are readily available. A taco is your typical food on the go. Once it's made, it does not last long as it is often immediately eaten; like pancakes. Then again, lots of Mexican American tacos are actually adaptations of Mexican food to the ingredients that can be obtained through the U.S. food-processing industry. This is one of the reasons you have tomato and cheddar cheese incorporated into the diet of Mexican-Americans.

Affordable, portable and convenient, a taco simply is a folded tortilla with some kind of filling. It is a very versatile dish as virtually anything can be enclosed in a soft or crispy tortilla — some appealing sauce or some crispy onions. The fact is tacos can be filled with the most delightful ingredients: pulled pork, various fresh veggies, chicken, chipotle-rubbed salmon or fried avocados. They can also be complemented with some popular toppings like salsa, onions, guacamole and cilantro.

Real tacos are prepared with homemade corn or flour tortillas, and they can be more than just a quick weeknight dinner when prepared fresh and with lots of fun. This book has been written to help you enjoy some good tacos within the comfort of your home. It includes 100 flavorful tacos from all over Mexico and beyond. There are plenty of fillings included in this recipe book to make for a simple and enjoyable meal. There are lots of options for vegetarians as well.

So why spend money eating tacos which may not be the real deal when you can actually make several delicious tacos of different variations in the comfort of your home. You get to save some money, as well. It may seem a bit challenging at first, but it's actually fun.

Let's do this!

Flour Tortillas

Enjoy the taste of freshly- made flour tortillas prepared in your home!

 Preparation time: 15 minutes

Cooking time: 45 minutes

Servings: 24

Ingredients:

4 cups of all-purpose flour

1 teaspoon of salt

2 teaspoons of baking powder

2 tablespoons of lard

1 1/2 cups of water

Directions:

1. In a mixing bowl, add the flour, salt and baking powder. Whisk it all together.

2. Add the lard using your fingers and mix until the flour looks like cornmeal.

3. Pour in the water and mix everything until they come together.

4. Lightly flour a surface and set the dough on it. Knead for a few minutes until it is elastic and smooth. Cut the dough into 24 pieces of equal size. Roll each of the pieces into a ball.

5. Over medium-high heat, preheat a big skillet. Using a rolling pin that is well-floured, roll a dough ball into a thin and round tortilla.

6. Put the round tortilla into the preheated skillet and allow to cook until its color becomes golden and it is bubbling. Flip to the other side and keep cooking until it is also golden.

7. Remove and keep in a tortilla warmer. Repeat the process for the other dough balls.

Corn Tortillas

With just two ingredients, you can make the most delicious tortillas.

Preparation time: 20 minutes

Cooking time: 15 minutes

Servings: 15

Ingredients:

1 3/4 cups of masa harina

1 1/8 cups of hot water

Directions:

1. Mix the ingredients thoroughly in a medium-sized bowl. Put the dough on a clean surface and knead until it is smooth and pliable. Cover it tightly with a plastic wrap and leave to stand for 30 minutes.

2. Over medium-high heat, preheat a cast iron pan.

3. Cut the dough into 15 balls of equal sizes. With your hands or a rolling pin, press each ball flat between two sheets of plastic wrap.

4. Put the tortilla in the pan immediately and cook for about 30 seconds or until it is browned and a bit puffy. Turn the tortilla on its other side and brown for about 30 seconds. Remove and put on a plate. Continue this method for the other balls.

Whole Wheat Tortillas

Another great recipe for you to try.

Preparation time: 10 minutes

Cooking time: 5 minutes

Servings: 10

Ingredients:

2 cups of whole wheat flour

1 teaspoon of baking powder

1/2 teaspoon of salt

2 tablespoons of olive oil

1/2 cup of warm water

Directions:

1. Mix the flour, baking powder and salt in a bowl. Add the olive oil and stir until it is mixed thoroughly.

2. Add the water using a few tablespoons per time. Do this until you can easily gather the dough into a ball.

3. Using your hands, knead the dough on a floured surface for about 10-15 minutes. Cover and allow to stand for 15 minutes.

4. Divide the dough into 10 balls of roughly equal size. Roll each of the balls into a circle.

5. Cook each of the tortillas in an ungreased pan for about 1 minute over medium-high heat 30 seconds per side. Cook the tortillas until they are puffy.

Mexican Tortillas

Tortillas made using the traditional Mexican recipe.

Preparation time: 30 minutes

Cooking time: 25 minutes

Servings: 12

Ingredients

3 cups of all-purpose flour

2 teaspoons of baking powder

2 teaspoons of salt

3/4 cup of shortening

3/4 cup of hot water

Directions:

1. Mix together the flour, baking powder and salt. Using your hand or a pastry cutter, cut in the shortening until the mixture becomes crumbly. Add

about 3/4 cup of water to it or just about enough water to make the mixture look moist.

2. Knead the dough with either your hand or a big fork until it forms a soft ball. Cover with a dish towel and allow to stand for about 60 minutes or thereabout.

3. Divide the dough into 12 balls. Roll each of the balls on a lightly floured surface using a rolling pin, to about 1/8-inch thickness.

4. Set each tortilla on a medium hot cast iron pan. Cook the tortilla on each side for about 1-2 minutes.

Easy-Peasy Tortillas

Very easy! Almost anybody can make this.

Preparation time: 24 minutes

Cooking time: 16 minutes

Servings: 8

Ingredients:

2 cups of all-purpose flour

1/2 teaspoon of salt

3/4 cup of water

3 tablespoons of olive oil

Directions:

1. Mix the flour and salt in a large bowl. Stir in water and oil. Knead 10-12 times on a floured surface. Add a little flour or water if necessary to get a smooth dough. Leave to stand for 10 minutes.

2. Divide the dough into 8 parts and roll each part into a 7-inch circle on a lightly floured surface.

3. Coat a large non-stick pan with cooking spray. Cook the tortillas for 1 minute per side over medium heat or until they are lightly browned. Keep the tortillas warm.

BEEF

Beef And Pineapple Tacos

A delicious and healthy meal served in no time at all.

Preparation time: 30 minutes

Cooking time: 0 minutes

Servings: 4

Ingredients:

1 pound of skirt steak, cut into 3 pieces

Kosher salt

¼ teaspoon of black pepper

1 tablespoon of olive oil

2 cups of chopped pineapple

½ red chili, chopped

8 corn tortillas

Cilantro

Lime wedges

Directions:

1. Season the beef with a teaspoon of salt and ¼ teaspoon of pepper. In a big pan, heat the olive oil over medium-high heat. Add the steak and cook for 2-3 minutes on each side or until it is done. Remove from the pan and slice the cooked beef.

2. Cook the pineapple and chili pepper in the pan for 6-8 minutes until it is soft. Toss frequently.

3. Divide equally and add the pineapple and steak to the tortillas.

4. Add the cilantro and lime wedges and serve.

Texas Beef Tacos

Delicious tacos from Texas.

Preparation time: 20 minutes

Cooking time: 25 minutes

Servings: 12

Ingredients:

1 tablespoon of corn oil

½ cup of chopped onion

½ cup of chopped green bell pepper

3 cloves of garlic, diced

1 ½ tablespoons of ground cumin

1 pound of lean ground beef

½ cup of tomato sauce

¼ cup of raisins

¼ cup of pecan pieces

¼ cup of chopped fresh cilantro

12 taco shells

Lettuce, shredded

Cheddar cheese, grated

Fresh tomatoes, diced

Salsa, store-bought

Directions:

1. In a heavy and large pan over medium-high heat, heat the corn oil. Sauté the onion, bell pepper and garlic for about 5 minutes until it is tender. Add the ground cumin and stir for 60 seconds.

2. Add the beef and cook for 10 minutes until it is browned, using the back of a fork to break up the beef. Scoop off the fat from the pan.

3. Add the tomato sauce, raisins and pecans to the pan. Cook for about 5 minutes until it is well heated while stirring frequently. Add the cilantro and mix together. Add salt and pepper to season.

4. Top the taco shell with ¼ cup of the filling, garnish with the lettuce, cheese, tomatoes and salsa.

Ground Beef Tacos

Preparation time: 5 minutes

Cooking time: 25 minutes

Servings: 6

Ingredients:

1 pound of lean ground beef

1 medium-sized onion, diced

1 teaspoon of chili powder

½ teaspoon of salt

½ teaspoon of garlic powder

1 (8-ounce) can of tomato sauce

12 taco shells

1 ½ cups of shredded cheese

2 cups of shredded lettuce

2 tomatoes, diced

¾ cup of salsa

Directions:

1. Preheat the oven to 250°F. Brown the beef and onion for 8-10 minutes in a medium-sized pan or until the beef is well cooked. Stir regularly and drain when cooked.

2. Add the chili powder, salt, garlic powder and tomato sauce and stir. Turn down the heat to low. Cover the pan and let it simmer 10 min.

3. In the meantime, set the taco shells on a cookie sheet that has not been greased and heat it for 5 minutes at 250F.

4. To serve, layer the beef, cheese, lettuce and tomatoes in each of the taco shell.

Serve with the salsa and add sour cream as toppings.

Crockpot Shredded Beef Tacos

Easy, stress-free and enough for the whole family.

Preparation time: 10 minutes

Cooking time: 8 hours

Servings: 22-25

Ingredients:

2-3 pounds of chuck roast

Salt

Pepper

1 teaspoon of cayenne

1 teaspoon of ground cumin

1 teaspoon of smoked paprika

1 teaspoon of garlic, diced

¼ cup of beef broth

2 tablespoons of tomato paste

1 jalapeno pepper, chopped

¼ cup of lime juice

1 medium-sized yellow onion, chopped

Directions:

1. Add salt and pepper to the beef to season. Brown the beef in a skillet for 2 minutes on each side over medium-high heat. Transfer to a plate and keep aside.

2. Mix the cayenne, cumin, paprika, garlic and beef broth. Add the tomato paste, jalapeno and lime juice. Stir everything together.

3. Put the beef in a crockpot and add the onions.

4. Pour the beef broth mixture over the beef in the crockpot and cook for 6-8 hours on low or 3-4 hours on high.

5. Use two forks to shred the beef when it is cooked and coat it with the juices by tossing.

6. Dish on the taco shells and serve hot with any toppings of your choice.

Steak Tacos

Enjoy the taste of steak with radishes, cilantro and cheese.

Preparation time: 10 minutes

Cooking time: 10 minutes

Servings: 8

Ingredients:

2 tablespoons of vegetable oil, divided

1 pound of skirt or flank steak

Kosher salt

Freshly ground pepper

1/2 cup of fresh cilantro leaves with soft stems, divided

2 spring onions, white and light green parts only, sliced thinly

4 radishes, trimmed, chopped

1/2 jalapeño, seeds removed (for less heat), chopped finely

2 tablespoons of fresh lime juice

8 corn tortillas, warmed

2 ounces of Cotija cheese or queso fresco, crumbled

Directions:

1. Season the steak with salt and pepper. In a big pan, heat a tablespoon of oil over high heat. Cook the steak for 5 minutes on each side until it is medium rare. Leave to stand for 5 minutes.

2. In the meantime, dice half of the cilantro and mix with the onions, radishes, jalapeno, lime juice and the rest of the oil in a medium-sized bowl. Add salt and pepper to season.

3. Slice the steak and put on the tortillas. Top it with the radish mixture, quesco fresco and the left-over cilantro.

Simple Beef Tacos
Making tacos does not get easier than this.

Preparation time: 15 minutes

Cooking time: 15 minutes

Servings: 10

Ingredients:

1 pound of lean ground beef

1 cup of salsa

10 taco shells

1/2 head of lettuce, shredded

1 medium-sized tomato, diced

1 cup of shredded cheddar cheese

Directions:

1. Brown the beef for 8-10 minutes in a 10-inch pan over medium heat. Stir occasionally. Drain when it is done.

2. Add the salsa to the beef and stir. Allow to boil while stirring continuously. Turn down the heat to medium low and cook for 5 minutes while stirring occasionally. Transfer the beef to a big serving bowl.

3. Heat the taco shells and top with the beef mixture, lettuce, tomato and cheese.

Crockpot Beef Tacos

A nutritious and sumptuous beef taco meal.

Preparation time: 10 minutes

Cooking time: 3 hours

Servings: 8

Ingredients:

2 pounds of lean ground beef

1 tablespoon of cumin

2 teaspoon of kosher salt

2 teaspoon of chili powder

2 teaspoon of paprika

1 teaspoon of dried oregano

1 small onion, diced

2 garlic cloves minced garlic

1/4 cup of crushed red bell pepper

1 cup of tomato sauce

1 bay leaf

16 corn taco shells

For the Toppings:

2 cups of shredded romaine lettuce

1 cup of shredded cheddar

2 plum tomatoes, chopped

Directions:

1. Heat a big non-stick pan over high heat and brown the beef. Break the beef into little pieces while it cooks.

2. Add 2 teaspoons of the cumin, the other spices, onion, bell pepper and garlic to the browned beef. Stir everything and cook until it is tender for 2-3 minutes.

3. Put the beef in a crockpot, add 1/2 cup of water and the tomato sauce. Cover and cook for 3 hours on high or 6-8 hours on low. Remove the bay leaf and add the rest of the cumin.

4. Heat the taco shells following package instructions.

5. To serve, put 1/4 cup of the beef in each of the shell and top with lettuce, a tablespoon of cheese and tomato.

Spicy Beef Tacos

Spicy, filling and very easy to make.

Preparation time: 12 minutes

Cooking time: 13 minutes

Servings: 4

Ingredients:

2 cloves of garlic, crushed

3/4 pound of raw 93% lean ground beef

1 1/2 teaspoon of ground coriander

1 1/2 teaspoon of ground cumin

3/4 teaspoon table salt

1 1/2 cups of canned diced tomatoes with peppers

8 small-sized corn tortillas, toasted lightly

2 cups of shredded lettuce

1/2 cup of low fat shredded cheddar cheese, sharp-variety

1/3 cup of no-fat salsa

Directions:

1. Grease a big pan with cooking spray and heat over medium-high heat. Sauté the garlic for about 30 seconds while stirring until it is aromatic.

2. Add the beef and cook for about 5-6 minutes until it turns brown. Break up the meat as it cooks.

3. Add the coriander, cumin, salt and the diced tomatoes and cook for 5-6minutes until all the liquid is almost absorbed. Stir occasionally.

4. Set the tortillas on a surface. Put about 1/4 cup of beef, 1/4 cup of lettuce, a tablespoon of cheese and 2 teaspoons of salsa on each of the tortillas. Fold in half and serve.

Jamaican Beef Tacos With Fruity Slaw

A dish appealing to all 5 senses!

Preparation time: 20 minutes

Cooking time: 50 minutes

Servings: 5

Ingredients:

For Slaw:

1/2 cup of chopped mango

1/2 cup of chopped fresh pineapple

1/2 cup chopped red onion

3 small-sized radishes, sliced thin

1/3 cup of fresh cilantro leaves and tender stems

2/3 cup of thinly sliced red cabbage

1 1/2 tablespoons of fresh lime juice

1/4 teaspoon of sugar

Kosher salt

For Beef Filling:

1 tablespoon of vegetable oil

4 scallions, white and pale green parts only, sliced thinly

1 small-sized yellow onion, chopped finely

4 medium-sized garlic cloves, crushed

1/2 or 1 Scotch bonnet pepper, seeded and diced, or Scotch bonnet hot sauce

1/2 teaspoon of paprika

1/4 teaspoon of allspice

1 teaspoon of Jamaican curry powder

1 teaspoon of dried thyme

1 pound of ground beef

1 teaspoon kosher salt, with extra for seasoning

1 teaspoon of freshly ground black pepper, with extra for seasoning

1 teaspoon of sugar

For Tortillas:

1 1/2 tablespoons of vegetable oil

1/4 teaspoon of turmeric powder

1/2 teaspoon of Jamaican curry powder

10 small flour tortillas

Directions:

1. For slaw: Toss all the slaw ingredients in a big bowl and keep in the refrigerator until it is time to serve.

2. For Beef Filling: In a big pan over medium high, heat the oil until it is shimmery. Add the scallions, yellow onion, garlic and scotch bonnet. Cook for about 4 minutes until the onions are tender and transparent while stirring occasionally. Stir in the paprika, allspice, curry powder and thyme.

3. Add the ground beef and as it cooks break up large chunks of it. When the beef starts to brown, add just about enough water to cover the meat. Add salt, pepper and sugar.

4. Let the beef boil, then reduce the heat to allow it simmer slowly. Simmer for about 25-30 minutes until the meat is well-done and the broth is saucy. Add salt and pepper to season.

5. For Tortillas: Mix thoroughly the oil, turmeric and curry powder in a small bowl. Using a baking sheet, brush oil on both sides of each of the tortillas.

6. Cook the tortillas one at a time for 2 minutes per side in a pan over moderate heat until the oil is absorbed and the tortillas are a bit crisp and still pliable. Transfer to a baking sheet and keep warm by covering it with a clean dish towel.

7. To serve, fill the tortillas with the cooked beef topping it with the pineapple slaw.

Serve warm.

Beef Tacos With Mango-Avocado Salsa

This fresh and filling recipe is perfect for the summer!

Preparation time: 15 minutes

Cooking time: 15 minutes

Servings: 11

Ingredients:

For the Beef Filling:

2 pounds of ground beef chuck

2 (10-ounce) cans of tomatoes with green chilies with their juice

1 teaspoon of chili powder, with extra for serving

1 teaspoon of kosher salt

For the Salsa:

1 mango, chopped

1 medium-sized avocado, chopped

1/ 2 medium-sized red onion, finely chopped

1/2 bunch of fresh cilantro, chopped

Juice from 1 medium-sized lime

1/4 teaspoon of salt

A pinch of black pepper

Others:

22 small-sized yellow corn tortillas

½ medium-sized iceberg lettuce, shredded

Sour cream

2 limes divided into wedges

Cilantro sprigs

Directions:

1. For the salsa: Mix the mango, avocado, red onion and cilantro in a bowl. Drizzle the lime juice over it. Sprinkle salt and pepper to season. Combine everything by tossing well. Set aside in the refrigerator until it is time to serve.

2. For the Beef Filling: Over medium-high heat, heat a big nonstick pan and add the ground beef. Cook for 5 minutes while stirring occasionally. When it is well-cooked, scoop the excess fat with a spoon and discard. Remain about 2-3 tablespoons in the skillet.

3. Add the cans of tomatoes, chili powder and kosher salt. Keep cooking for 7-10 minutes until the beef is well-cooked, the sauce is reduced slightly and majority of the tomato liquid has been absorbed.

4. Heat both sides of the tortillas for 15-30 seconds on each side, in a dry big nonstick pan over medium-high heat. Transfer to a plate and keep warm by covering with a foil.

5. Put a spoonful of beef on each tortilla, top with the lettuce, salsa, cilantro sprigs, sour cream and an optional sprinkle of chili powder. Squeeze the fresh lime juice over it, serve.

CHICKEN

Chicken Tacos

This dish is easy to make and satisfying for everyone.

Preparation time: 20 minutes

Cooking time: 20 minutes

Servings: 6-12

Ingredients:

1 pound of halved chicken breasts, skinless, boneless and cut into bite-sized pieces

1 cup of lemonade

2 tablespoons of olive oil

1 tablespoon of lime juice

1 1/2 teaspoons of Worcestershire sauce

1/2 teaspoon of garlic powder

1/2 teaspoon of onion powder

1 bay leaf

1 (12-ounce) package of corn tortillas

1 head of lettuce, shredded

2 large-sized tomatoes, diced

1 (8-ounce) package of shredded Cheddar cheese, sharp variety

1 (8-ounce) jar of salsa

1 (8-ounce) container of sour cream

Directions:

1. Combine the chicken, lemonade, olive oil, lime juice and Worcestershire sauce in a big pan. Add the garlic powder, onion powder and bay leaf to season. Simmer for 15-20 minutes until the color is no longer pink and the juices are clear. Transfer to a serving bowl when done.

2. In the meantime, warm the tortillas until they are soft but pliable in either an oven or a microwave.

3. To serve, put the lettuce, tomatoes, cheese, salsa and sour cream in different dishes. Allow each person make their own preferred tacos with the ingredients of their choice.

Grilled Chicken Tacos

A recipe suitable for those busy weeknights.

Preparation time: 5 minutes

Cooking time: 8 minutes

Servings: 4

Ingredients:

2 cloves of garlic, chopped finely

1 medium-sized onion, cut into wedges, with its root intact

1 tablespoon of cumin seeds, roughly crushed

1 pound of chicken thighs, boneless, skinless

1 tablespoon of vegetable oil

1 teaspoon of kosher salt

1/2 teaspoon of freshly ground black pepper

For Serving:

8 corn tortillas, warmed

2 avocados, sliced

Salsa verde

Cilantro sprigs

Sliced radishes

Lime wedges

Directions:

1. Preheat the grill on medium-high heat.

2. In a medium-sized bowl, combine the garlic, onion, cumin, chicken, oil, salt and pepper. Toss together.

3. Grill the onion and chicken for about 4 minutes per side until it is lightly charred and well-cooked. Allow the chicken to stand for 5 minutes before you slice.

4. Serve the chicken with the tortillas, avocados, salsa verde, cilantro, radishes and lime wedges.

Shredded Chicken Tacos

Also called Tinga de Pollo. This dish is simple and delicious.

Preparation time: 10 minutes

Cooking time: 40 minutes

Servings: 4

Ingredients:

2 (8-ounce each) cans of Tomato Sauce

2 teaspoons of White Distilled Vinegar

2 teaspoons of Crushed Garlic

3½ teaspoons of ancho chili powder

1 teaspoon of Ground Cumin

2 teaspoons of Oregano Leaf

½ teaspoon of sugar

All-purpose Seasoning with Pepper

2 tablespoons of Extra Virgin Olive Oil

2 pounds of chicken breasts, bone-in, with skin

12 Corn Tortillas, heated

For Garnish (optional):

Avocadoes, chopped

Fresh cilantro, roughly chopped

Lettuce, shredded

Lime wedges

White onions, finely chopped

Tomatoes, chopped

Hot Sauce

Directions:

1. Combine the tomato sauce, vinegar, garlic, chili powder, cumin, oregano and sugar in a medium-sized bowl. Add the all-purpose seasoning and keep aside.

2. In a big pan, heat oil over medium-high heat, season the chicken with the all-purpose seasoning and place in the pan. Cook for about 5 minutes until it turns light golden brown on both sides. Turn only once.

3. Add the tomato sauce mixture to the pan and allow to boil. Reduce the heat to medium low. Cover and simmer for about 20 minutes until the chicken is well-done. Flip only once.

4. Transfer the chicken to a chopping board and reserve the sauce in the skillet. Remove and dispose of the bones and skin. Shred the chicken with two forks.

5. Return the shredded chicken to the pan containing the sauce. Mix everything together. Keep cooking for about an extra 10 minutes until the sauce is lessened, blends with the chicken and the mixture starts to caramelize.

6. Spoon the chicken on the tortillas, garnish with preferred toppings and serve.

Crockpot Shredded Chicken Tacos

A yummy and easy-to-prepare treat.

Preparation time: 10 minutes

Cooking time: 6 hours

Servings: 4

Ingredients:

1 cup of chicken broth

3 tablespoons of taco seasoning mix

1 pound of chicken breasts, skinless, boneless

Directions:

1. Mix together the chicken broth and taco seasoning in a bowl. Put the chicken breasts in a crockpot and pour the broth-taco mixture over it.

2. Cover and cook for 6-8 hours on low.

3. Serve with your preferred taco or tortillas.

Mexican Grilled Chicken Tacos

Made with inspiration from Sinaloa chicken, a popular Mexican street food.

Preparation time: 5 minutes

Cooking time: 10 minutes

Servings: 4-5

Ingredients:

1 - 1.5 lb chicken thigh fillets

1 tablespoon of olive oil

<u>For the Marinade:</u>

4 tablespoons of orange juice

2 tablespoons of apple cider vinegar

1½ tablespoons of lime juice

3 cloves of garlic, minced

1½ tablespoons of chipotle or ancho chile powder

2 teaspoons of dried oregano

2 teaspoons of smoked paprika powder

⅛ tsp All-Spice

¼ teaspoon of cinnamon powder

¼ - ½ teaspoon of cayenne pepper, optional

1 teaspoon of salt

Black pepper

<u>For the Serving:</u>

Tortillas or taco shells

Tomato salsa

Sour cream

Avocado

Fresh coriander or cilantro

Lime wedges

Directions:

1. Combine all the ingredients for the marinade in a Ziploc bag.

2. Add the chicken, coat with the ingredients by rubbing it and refrigerate for at least 3 hours or overnight preferably, in order for it to marinate. Remove the chicken and dispose of the marinade.

3. In a pan, heat oil over medium high heat and cook the chicken for 4 minutes per side until it turns dark golden brown.

4. Transfer to a plate, cover it with foil loosely and leave to rest for 3 minutes.

5. Cut the chicken into strips and serve on the tacos or tortillas.

Pulled Chicken Tacos

Colorful, amazing, flavorful!

Preparation time: 30 minutes

Cooking time: 40 minutes

Servings: 8

Ingredients:

For chicken:

2 teaspoons of olive oil

3 large chicken breasts, skin-on, bone-in

1 cup of chicken broth

1 (16-ounce) can of tomato sauce

1 tablespoon of chili powder

1 teaspoon of garlic powder

1 teaspoon of oregano

1 teaspoon of cumin

½ teaspoon of sugar

½ teaspoon of salt

¼ teaspoon of pepper

For Salsa:

1 cup of pineapple, finely chopped

½ cup of red bell pepper, finely chopped

2 tablespoons of red onion, finely crushed

Juice from 1 lime

½ cup of loosely packed cilantro leaves, finely chopped

Salt

For Cilantro Sauce:

1 cup of sour or light cream

½ cup of fresh cilantro leaves, coarsely chopped

2 teaspoons of lime juice

1½ teaspoons of honey

¼ cup of prepared green salsa

Salt

Pepper

1 cup of finely shredded purple cabbage

8 corn tortillas

Garnish (optional):

Lime wedges

Cilantro leaves

Directions:

1. For Salsa: Mix all the salsa ingredients in a bowl and keep aside in the refrigerator until time of serving.

2. For Chicken: Mix together the chicken broth, tomato sauce, chili powder, garlic powder, oregano, cumin, salt, sugar and pepper in a bowl.

3. Season the chicken with salt and pepper. Heat the oil in a large pan over medium high heat. Set the chicken with its skin side facing down and cook until it is golden brown for 4-6 minutes per side.

4. Remove pan from heat then pour the tomato sauce mixture on the chicken. Return the pan to the heat and allow the sauce mixture to boil. Cover and turn down the heat to low. Simmer until the chicken is well-done for 35 minutes.

5. Remove and discard the skin and bones from the chicken. Using two forks, shred the meat. Pour the rest of the sauce in the pan over the shredded meat and toss to coat. Add salt and pepper to taste.

6. Put the chicken and tomato sauce mix in a slow cooker and cook on high for 4 hours or low for 8 hours.

7. For Cilantro Sauce: Put all the ingredients in a food processor and blend together until it is smooth.

8. To serve, divide the cabbage equally among the tortillas and top each with 1/4 cup of chicken, a tablespoon of salsa and a drizzle of the cilantro sauce. Garnish with the lime wedges and cilantro leaves.

Spicy Baked Chicken Tacos

Hot and easy to prepare.

Preparation time: 15 minutes

Cooking time: 15 minutes

Servings: 4-5

Ingredients:

1 tablespoon of olive oil

1/2 pound of cooked chicken, shredded

1 ounce of hot and spicy taco seasoning

1/2 cup of onion, chopped

4 1/2 ounces of diced green chilies

14 1/2 ounces of diced tomatoes, drained

10 taco shells

8 ounces of refried beans

2 cups of Mexican blend cheese, shredded

Jalapeno

Sour cream

Salsa

Cilantro

Lettuce, shredded

Directions:

1. Preheat the oven to 400°F. Grease a 13x9-inch baking dish with nonstick cooking spray and keep aside.

2. In a medium-sized skillet, heat the olive oil over medium heat. Sauté the onion until it turns translucent and aromatic for 2-3 minutes.

3. Add the chicken, taco seasoning, tomatoes and green chilies. Mix together and turn down the heat to allow it simmer. Cook for 5-8 minutes.

4. Set the taco shells in the baking dish, upright. Put a tablespoon of beans at the bottom of each shell and top with the chicken mixture, almost to the top of each of the shell. Sprinkle the shredded cheese on each shell generously.

5. Put in the oven and bake for 12-14 minutes until the cheese melts and the shells' edges are browned.

6. Remove, top with jalapenos, sour cream, cilantro and salsa. Serve.

Chicken Soft Tacos

This recipe is quick and quite easy to make.

Preparation time: 5 minutes

Cooking time: 5 minutes

Servings: 6

Ingredients:

1 rotisserie cooked chicken, boneless, skinless, cut into bite-sized pieces

2 (7-ounce each) cans of salsa verde

1 (15-ounce) can of black beans or pinto beans

1 cup of shredded Mexican blend cheese

11/2 teaspoons of Mexican seasoning

12 corn tortillas

Directions:

1. Put the chicken in a medium-sized pan with the salsa verde and seasoning.

2. Cook for 5 minutes over medium heat until it is warmed.

3. Heat the tortillas. Spoon the chicken into the tortillas and add beans and cheese as toppings.

Spicy Chicken Tacos

Nothing like a little spice to liven up those boring weeknights.

Preparation time: 20 minutes

Cooking time: 35 minutes

Servings: 4

Ingredients:

8 corn tortillas

1 pound of chicken breasts, boneless, skinless, fat removed and cut into thin strips

1/4 teaspoon of salt

2 teaspoons of canola oil, divided

1 large-sized onion, chopped

1 large-sized green bell pepper, seeded and chopped

3 large-sized garlic cloves, crushed

1 jalapeño pepper, seeded and crushed

1 tablespoon of ground cumin

1/2 cup of prepared hot salsa, with extra for garnish

1/4 cup of diced fresh cilantro

Scallions, sliced

Fresh tomatoes, chopped
Low-fat sour cream

Directions:

1. Preheat the oven to 300°F. Use foil to wrap the tortillas and bake for 10-15 minutes until they are well-heated.

2. In the meantime, season the chicken with salt. In a big and heavy skillet, heat a teaspoon of oil over high heat until it is extremely hot.

3. Add the chicken and ensure it is browned on all sides for about 6 minutes. Remove and put in a bowl.

4. Turn down the heat to medium and add the rest of the oil to the pan. Sauté the onion for 3-5 minutes while stirring until it begins to brown around the edges.

5.Add the bell pepper, garlic, jalapeno and cumin and cook for an extra 2-3 minutes while stirring until the peppers turn bright green.

6. Add the salsa and chicken. Cook for about 2 minutes until the chicken is well-done while stirring continuously. Bring down from the heat and stir in the cilantro.

7. Put into the warmed tortillas and add scallions, tomatoes and sour cream as garnish.

Soft Chicken Tacos

Try your hands at Mexican cuisine with this simple recipe.

Preparation time: 5 minutes

Cooking time: 20 minutes

Servings: 4

Ingredients:

1 teaspoon of chili powder

1/2 teaspoon of salt

1/2 teaspoon of ground cumin

1/2 teaspoon of freshly ground black pepper

1 pound of chicken thighs, boneless and skinless

12 (6-inch) white corn tortillas

1 1/2 cups of thinly sliced green cabbage

1/4 cup of shredded low-fat Monterey Jack cheese

Reduced-fat sour cream, optional

Directions:

1. Mix the chili powder, salt, cumin and black pepper in a small bowl and rub over the chicken.

2. Grease the grill rack with a cooking spray and set the chicken on it. Grill for 10 minutes per side or until it is well cooked. Leave to stand for 5 minutes, and then chop.

3. Heat the tortillas following package instructions. Divide the chicken among the tortillas equally. Top each tortilla with a teaspoon of cheese and 2 tablespoons of cabbage. Serve with sour cream.

PORK

Crockpot Pork Tacos

Just a few steps result in these delicious tacos.

Preparation time: 25 minutes

Cooking time: 5 hour 11 minutes

Servings: 8

Ingredients:

3 whole ancho chilies

3 whole pasilla chilies

4 garlic cloves, unpeeled

1/2 medium-sized white onion, coarsely chopped

2-3 chipotles in adobo sauce

3 tablespoons of extra-virgin olive oil

1 tablespoon of cider vinegar

2 tablespoons of honey

Kosher salt

2 teaspoons of dried oregano

3 3/4 cups reduced-sodium chicken broth

4 pounds of pork shoulder, boneless, untrimmed, cut into chunks

Freshly ground pepper

2 bay leaves

1 cinnamon stick

Corn tortillas, warmed

Taco toppings, for garnish

Directions:

1. Place the ancho chilies, pasilpala chilies and garlic in a bowl. Add 2-3 tablespoons of water and microwave for 2-3 minutes on high until it is soft and pliable.

2. Remove the stems and seeds from the chilies, peel the garlic and transfer them to a blender. Add the onion, chipotles, 2 tablespoons olive oil, vinegar, honey, 1 tablespoon salt and the oregano and blend until it forms a smooth puree.

3. In a big skillet, heat the rest of the oil over high heat. Add the blended chili puree to the skillet and fry for about 8 minutes until it is thick and aromatic, stir continuously. Add the chicken broth and reduce until it thickens a bit.

4. Season the pork with salt and pepper and put in a big crockpot. Add the bay leaves and cinnamon stick. In the sauce, cover and cook for 5 hours on high until the pork is soft.

5. Remove and dispose of the bay leaves and cinnamon stick. Pour in the sauce, cover and cook for 5 hours on high until the pork is soft.

6. Put the shredded meat in the tortillas alongside your preferred toppings. Serve.

Lime Pork Tacos
Simple to prepare and packed with enough flavors to satiate your taste buds.

Preparation time: 10 minutes

Cooking time: 11 minutes

Servings: 4

Ingredients:

1 pound of pork tenderloin, trimmed, cut into thin strips

1/4 teaspoon of salt

1/8 teaspoon of freshly ground black pepper

2 teaspoons of olive oil

1 1/2 cups of thinly sliced onion

1 small-sized jalapeño pepper, seeded and diced

1/2 cup of no-fat, reduced-sodium chicken broth

1/2 cup of chopped plum tomato

3 tablespoons of chopped cilantro

2 1/2 tablespoons of fresh lime juice

8 (6-inch) flour tortillas

Directions:

1. Preheat a big nonstick pan over medium high heat. Season the pork with salt and black pepper. Add oil to the pan and sauté for 4 minutes until it is browned.

2. Add the onion and jalapeno to the pan and sauté for 5 minutes or until it is soft.

3. Pour in the chicken broth, turn down the heat and allow to simmer for a minute. Add in the tomato, stir and allow to simmer for 2 minutes.

4. Put the pork and its juices back into the pan. Add in the cilantro and lime juice, stir and cook for a minute or until the pork is cooked thoroughly.

5. Scoop 1/2 cup of the pork mixture into each of the tortillas and serve.

Slow Cooker Pulled Pork Tacos

This dish is filling and delicious.

Preparation time: 10 minutes

Cooking time: 8 hours

Servings: 6-8

Ingredients:

1 tablespoon of cumin

1 teaspoon of garlic powder

1 teaspoon of chili powder

1 teaspoon of onion powder

1 teaspoon of paprika

1 teaspoon of oregano

1 tablespoon of salt

1 (3-1/2 - 4 pounds) pork shoulder, rinsed and cleaned

1 (16-ounce) jar of mild salsa

1 package of corn or flour tortillas

Directions:

1. In a small bowl, combine the cumin, garlic powder, chili powder, onion powder, paprika, oregano and salt thoroughly.

2. Put the pork in the slow cooker and rub the seasoning mixture all over it. Pour the jar of salsa around the pork.

3. Cover and cook for 8-12 hours on low.

4. Transfer the pork to a plate and shred into bite-size pieces with two forks. Pour about a scoop or two of the juices over the pork and mix together.

5. Put the pork on the tortillas and serve with your preferred toppings.

Shredded Pork Tacos

A delicious recipe guaranteed to be a hit with anyone.

Preparation time: 30 minutes

Cooking time: 3 hours 45 minutes

Servings: 8

Ingredients:

1 tablespoon of olive oil

1 large-sized onion, diced

6 garlic cloves, crushed

1/2 teaspoon of dried thyme

1/4 teaspoon of dried oregano

2 bay leaves

Coarse salt

Ground pepper

3 tablespoons of tomato paste

1 (3-pound) pork shoulder, boneless, cut in half lengthwise

1 (28 ounces) can of whole tomatoes in juice

1 large-sized chipotle chili in adobo sauce, minced

16 (6-inch) corn tortillas, toasted

1 cup of crumbled feta, goat cheese or queso fresco

1 cup of fresh cilantro leaves

Directions:

1. Heat the olive oil in a big and heavy pot over medium heat. Add onion, garlic, thyme, oregano, bay leaves and season with salt and pepper.

2. Cook for about 5 minutes until the onion is soft. Stir in the tomato paste. Add the pork, tomatoes with their juice, chipotle and a cup of water. Allow to boil.

3. Turn down the heat, cover and simmer for 2-2 1/2 hours. Remove and dispose of the bay leaves.

4. Remove the meat with tongs to a big bowl. Using 2 forks, shred the meat and dispose of any big pieces of fat or gristle.

5. Put the meat back into the pan and simmer for 30-45 minutes until the sauce is thick. Add extra salt and pepper to season if required.

6. Put the pork and its sauce into the tortillas and top with the cheese and cilantro.

Fried Pork Tacos

Spicy, crispy and perfect for dinner.

Preparation time: 15 minutes

Cooking time: 15 minutes

Servings: 4-6

Ingredients:

1 ½ pounds of pork shoulder, cut into 1/2-inch strips

Salt

Pepper

3 cloves of garlic, finely chopped

2 ½ teaspoons of ground guajillo or ancho

1 teaspoon of toasted, roughly ground cumin

3 tablespoons of vegetable oil

2 dozen small-sized corn tortillas

Tomatillo salsa

Salsa cruda

Radishes, trimmed

Cilantro sprigs

Directions:

1. Season the pork with salt and pepper. Add garlic, chili powder and cumin to the seasoned pork. Mix together, using your fingers to rub the seasoning into the meat. Allow the meat to marinate for an hour at the very least, or refrigerate overnight.

2. In a large cast iron pan heat the oil over medium heat. Add the meat when the oil looks wavy and allow it to sizzle. Cook for 5-7 minutes until the pork is browned lightly and well-done while stirring occasionally. Remove from the heat and keep the pork warm.

3. Heat the tortillas on a cast iron pan that has not been greased.

4. To serve, put a little of the pork on the tortillas, top with a spoonful of tomatillo salsa and salsa cruda. Garnish with the radishes and cilantro sprigs. Serve!

Pork Tacos With Pineapple Salsa

A sweet, savory and spicy dish!

Preparation time: 15 minutes

Cooking time: 10 minutes

Servings: 6-8

Ingredients:

For Pork:

1 tablespoon of vegetable oil

1 shallot

1 garlic clove

1 jalapeno, ribbed and seeded

2 teaspoons of fish sauce

18 ounces of pork loin, boneless, sliced into thin strips

2 tablespoons of sugar

2 tablespoons of water

For Pineapple Salsa:

1 cup of diced pineapple

1 cup of diced cucumber

½ cup of diced cilantro

½ cup of diced red onion

A squeeze of lime juice

A pinch of salt

For Serving:

Tortillas

Cilantro

Lime

Chili sauce

Directions:

1. For The Pork: In a heavy skillet heat the oil over medium heat. Sauté the shallot, garlic, and jalapeño for about 2 minutes until it is fragrant.

2. Increase the heat and add pork and fish sauce to the skillet. Stir fry for some minutes until the pork loses its pink color.

3. While the heat is still high, add the sugar and water, stirring only once. (Do not stir the pork for about a minute for easy caramelization). Repeat this process until the pork is done and turns golden brown.

4. For Salsa: Combine all the salsa ingredients in a medium-sized bowl and toss everything together.

5. Quickly heat the tortillas in a greased pan. Divide the pork evenly among 6 tortillas and top with the salsa and chili sauce.

Ground Pork Tacos

Another easy way to use ground pork.

Preparation time: 5 minutes

Cooking time: 15 minutes

Servings: 4

Ingredients:

1 pound of ground pork

1 (8-ounce) can of diced tomatoes

1/2 cup of chopped onion

1 tablespoon of chili powder

1 tablespoon of garlic powder

8 flour tortillas

Garnish (optional)

Lettuce

Shredded cheese

Sour cream

Directions:

1. In a big pan, brown the pork.

2. Add the tomatoes with its liquid, onion, chili powder and garlic powder.

3. Allow to boil, then turn down the heat and let it simmer for 10minutes, until most of the liquid is absorbed while stirring occasionally.

4. Spoon the mixture into the tortillas, top with your preferred garnish and serve.

Pork Chops Taco

An improved version of the normal tacos.

Preparation time: 5 minutes

Cooking time: 8 minutes

Servings: 4

Ingredients:

4 pork loin chops, boneless

1 tablespoon of canola oil

1 (8-ounce) can of tomato sauce

1 cup of water, divided

1 medium-sized onion, chopped

1 envelope of taco seasoning

2 tablespoons of all-purpose flour

Directions:

1. Cook the pork chops in oil using a large pan over medium heat for 2-3 minutes per side or until it is browned lightly.

2. Mix the tomato sauce, 3/4 cup water, onion and taco seasoning in a small bowl. Pour the mixture over the pork and bring to a boil. Turn down the heat, cover and leave to simmer for 4-5 minutes. Leave the pork to stand for 5 minutes before serving. Transfer the pork to a serving plate and keep it warm.

3. Mix the flour and remaining water until it forms a smooth paste. Stir this mixture into the pan and bring to a boil. Cook and stir for 2 minutes or until the sauce becomes thick. Serve with the pork chops.

BBQ Pork And Onion Tacos

This recipe leaves you with a moist and yummy dish.

Preparation time: 5 minutes

Cooking time: 12 minutes

Servings: 4

Ingredients:

8 pork loin cutlets, 1/4-inch thick

1 large-sized sweet onion, cut crosswise into 1/2-inch thick rounds

2 tablespoons of extra virgin olive oil

Kosher salt

Freshly ground pepper

2 teaspoons of chili powder

8 (6-inch) flour or corn tortillas, warmed

1/2 cup of cilantro leaves

1 avocado, cut into halves and sliced lengthwise

Sour cream

Lime wedges

Directions:

1. Preheat the grill. Place the cutlets and onion on a large baking sheet. Coat all over with the oil and season with the salt and pepper. Season only the cutlets with the chili powder.

2. Over moderately high heat, grill the onions for about 8 minutes until it is charred and soft. Turn only once. Transfer to a chopping board and keep warm by covering with foil.

3. Grill the cutlets for about 2 minutes until they are just cooked through. Turn only once.

4. Remove the pork to the chopping board. Chop the onions roughly and cut the cutlets into 1/2-inch strips. Serve with tortillas, cilantro, avocado, sour cream and lime wedges.

Grilled Pork Tacos With Cilantro Slaw
A delicious and nutritious change from the norm.

Preparation time: 5 minutes

Cooking time: 28 minutes

Servings: 6

Ingredients:

6 (1-inch thick) pork chops, boneless

2 tablespoons of olive oil

1 teaspoon of kosher salt

1/2 teaspoon of freshly ground pepper

12 (6-inch) flour tortillas

Lime wedges

For the Cilantro Slaw:

1/2 small head napa cabbage, thinly sliced

1 (8-ounce) can of pineapple tidbits, drained

1/3 cup of thinly sliced green onions

1/3 cup of diced radishes

1/4 cup of thinly sliced sweet onion

1/4 cup of shredded carrot

1/4 cup of finely diced fresh cilantro

2 tablespoons of Champagne vinegar

1 tablespoon of olive oil

Directions:

1. Leave the meat to stand for 30-40 minutes at room temperature.

2. <u>For The Slaw</u>: Toss all the slaw ingredients in a bowl. Season with salt and pepper. Cover and chill 30 minutes.

3. Light one part of the grill and heat to 350-400F, leave the other part unlit. Coat the pork with olive oil and sprinkle it with salt and pepper.

4. Grill the pork over the lit part of the grill for 4 minutes per side, cover with the grill lid.

5. Transfer the pork to the unlit part, and grill for 10 minutes per side, cover with the grill lid. Allow to stand for 5 minutes then slice the pork thinly.

6. Warm the tortillas and place the pork in them, top with the slaw. Serve with lime wedges.

FISH & SEAFOODS

Fish Tacos

A wonderful meal great for the whole family.

Preparation time: 60 minutes

Cooking time: 10 minutes

Servings: 4

Ingredients:

1/2 red onion, thinly sliced

1 1/2 cups of red wine vinegar

1/4 cup of olive oil

1 1/2 teaspoons of ancho chili powder

1 1/2 teaspoons of dried oregano

1/2 teaspoon of ground cumin

1/4 cup of chopped cilantro leaves, and extra for garnish

1 jalapeño, stemmed and chopped

1 pound of flaky white fish, cut into 4 chunks

Salt

8 corn tortillas

Mexican crema

Fresh Tomato Salsa

2 small sized limes, cut into quarters

Directions:

1. Soak the onion in the red wine vinegar and allow to marinate for a minimum of 30 minutes or for up to a month.

2. Mix the jalapeno, cilantro, ancho chili, cumin, oregano and olive oil in a small bowl. Put the cut fish on a flat dish and pour the mixture over it. Ensure both sides of the fish are well coated with the marinade and set aside for 20 minutes.

3. Place a nonstick skillet over medium-high heat. Put the fish into the preheated skillet, season with salt and allow to cook for 4 minutes. Turn the fish over and cook for another 2 minutes.

4. Remove from heat and shred the fish into the skillet using a fork, stir and set aside.

5. Heat the tortillas in a microwave on medium for 45 seconds. Place a spoonful of the flaked fish in the middle of each tortilla, sprinkle with the marinated onions and garnish with the lime wedges. Serve with the crema and salsa.

Simple Fish Tacos

With just a few ingredients, your tacos are ready in no time.

Preparation time: 10 minutes

Cooking time: 40 minutes

Servings: 6

Ingredients

1 (10-12 ounces) package of breaded or battered fish fillets

1 (4.6 ounce) box of taco shells

1/2 cup of mayonnaise or salad dressing

1 (1 ounce) of taco seasoning mix

6 cups of coleslaw mix

Taco sauce, optional

Directions:

1. Bake the fish fillets according to the instructions on the package. When it is done, cut each of the fillets into bite-size pieces.

2. Heat the taco shells in the oven following the directions on the box.

3. Mix the mayonnaise and seasoning mix in a medium-sized bowl and stir in the coleslaw mixture. Leave it to stand for 5 minutes.

4. To serve, spoon the fish pieces and coleslaw mixture onto the taco shells and top with the taco sauce.

Grilled Fish Tacos

A healthy alternative to frying the fish.

Preparation time: 30 minutes

Cooking time: 10 minutes

Servings: 6

Ingredients:

For the Fish:

4 teaspoons of chili powder

2 tablespoons of lime juice

2 tablespoons of extra virgin olive oil

1 teaspoon of ground cumin

1 teaspoon of onion powder

1 teaspoon of garlic powder

1 teaspoon of salt

1/2 teaspoon of freshly ground pepper

2 pounds of Pacific halibut, skinned, 1/2-3/4 inch thick and cut into 4 portions

For the Coleslaw:

1/4 cup of low-fat mayonnaise

1/4 cup of low-fat sour cream

2 tablespoons of chopped fresh cilantro

2 tablespoons of lime juice

1 teaspoon of lime zest

1 teaspoon of sugar

1/8 teaspoon of salt

Freshly ground pepper

3 cups of finely shredded red or green cabbage

12 corn tortillas, warmed

Directions:

1. For the fish: In a small bowl, mix together the chili powder, lime juice, oil, cumin, onion powder, garlic powder, salt and pepper. Rub this mixture all over the fish. Leave it for 20-30 minutes so that the fish can absorb the flavor.

2. For the coleslaw: In a medium-sized bowl mix together the mayonnaise, sour cream, cilantro, lime juice, lime zest, sugar, salt and pepper until it is smooth and creamy. Add the cabbage to the mixture and toss to combine. Refrigerate until it is time to serve.

3. Preheat the grill to medium-high. Grease the grill rack and grill the fish for 3-5 minutes on each side until it is well-cooked and can be easily flaked with a fork. Remove the fish to a platter and separate it into large chunks.

4. Serve the fish on the tacos topped with the coleslaw and garnishes.

Mexican Fish Tacos

Have a taste of Mexico without leaving your house.

Preparation time: 10 minutes

Cooking time: 10 minutes

Servings: 4

Ingredients:

2 cups of packaged shredded cabbage or coleslaw mix

3/4 cup of salsa, divided

2 tablespoon of sour cream

1 pound of halibut or tilapia fish fillets, cut into 1/2-inch thick strips.

1 teaspoon of chili powder

2 teaspoon of vegetable oil

8 (6-inch) corn tortillas, warmed

2 (8 ounce) of Mexican Cheese

Lime wedges (optional)

Directions:

1. Mix the cabbage, 1/4 cup salsa and sour cream thoroughly in a medium-sized bowl and set aside.

2. Sprinkle the chili powder over the fillets. In a large nonstick pan heat the oil over medium heat until hot. Add the fillets and cook for 2-3 minutes on each side or until the fish turns opaque in the center.

3. Fill the warmed tortillas with the fillets, half of the cheese, left-over 1/2 cup salsa, cabbage mix and the remaining cheese. Serve with lime wedges if needed.

Slow Cooker Fish Tacos

These tacos are made with cilantro and lime which brings the flavors together.

Preparation time: 5 minutes

Cooking time: 4 hours

Servings: 6

Ingredients:

6 frozen tilapia fillets

1 can of diced tomatoes, drained

1/2 teaspoon of crushed garlic

1 1/2 tablespoons of dried cilantro or 1/4 cup of fresh chopped cilantro

2 tablespoons of lime juice

Salt

Soft taco shells

Directions:

1. Put the frozen fillets in the bottom of the slow cooker.

2. Add the tomatoes, garlic, cilantro, lime juice, and salt. Cover and cook on low for 4 hours.

3. Use a fork to flake the fish and combine with the other ingredients. Spoon into the taco shells.

Grilled Shredded Tilapia Tacos

Citrus-infused tacos served with nutritious spicy slaw.

Preparation time: 18 minutes

Cooking time: 6 minutes

Servings: 6

Ingredients:

1 tablespoon of ground chipotle seasoning

1 1/2 teaspoons of ground cumin

1/2 teaspoon of salt

6 (6-ounce) tilapia fillets

2 tablespoons of olive oil

1 teaspoon of grated lime rind

2 tablespoons of fresh lime juice

12 corn tortillas

For slaw:

1 cup of reduced-fat sour cream

2 tablespoons of rice wine vinegar

2 tablespoons of pineapple

1/2 teaspoon of salt

1/4-1/2 teaspoon of dried chipotle seasoning

1 (16-ounce) package of cabbage slaw mix

Fresh lime wedges, garnish

Directions:

1. For the slaw: In a medium bowl combine the sour cream, vinegar, pineapple, salt and seasoning together. Add the slaw mix and toss everything to coat. Keep in the refrigerator until it is time to serve.

2. For the fillets: Mix together the chipotle seasoning, cumin and salt in a small bowl. Rub this mixture over the fillets evenly.

3. Mix together the olive oil, grated rind, and juice in a small bowl and rub over the fillets.

4. Grease the grill basket with a cooking spray and arrange the fillets in it.

5. Grill the fillets over medium-high heat for 3 minutes per side or just until the fish starts to flake with a fork. Cool it slightly before shredding the fish.

6. Spoon 2-3 tablespoons of the fillets into the tortillas and top with the slaw. Serve the taco with a squeeze of fresh lime juice.

Shrimp Tacos With Avocado Salsa

Crunchy taco loaded with avocado salsa verde.

Preparation time: 30 minutes

Cooking time: 10 minutes

Servings: 4

Ingredients:

For Salsa:

1 small onion, cut into quarters

1 jalapeno, cut into quarters, seeded

1 clove of garlic, crushed

4 medium tomatillos, husked, rinsed, and roughly chopped

65

1/2 Hass avocado, peeled, seeded, and cut into chunks

1 1/4 teaspoons of kosher salt

1/4 cup of loosely packed fresh cilantro leaves, roughly chopped

For Shrimp:

1 tablespoon of olive oil

1 teaspoon of chipotle

1 teaspoon of kosher salt

1 pound of medium shrimp, peeled, deveined

8 corn tortillas

8 sprigs of cilantro, as garnish

2 limes, cut into wedges

Directions:

1. In a food processor put the onion, jalapeno and garlic. Chop them finely. Add tomatillos, avocado, and salt and pulse until they are chopped but still chunky. Remove to a bowl, add in the cilantro and stir.

2. Preheat a grill to medium-high. In a big bowl, mix together the olive oil, chipotle or chili powder, and salt. Add the shrimp to the mixture and toss to coat. Grill the shrimp for about 1 1/2-2 minutes until it turns translucent.

3. Grill the tortillas for about 20 seconds on each side, until they are slightly charred and pliable. Spoon the sauce onto the grilled tortilla, then top with about 2 or 3 shrimp, a sprig of cilantro and a lime wedge on the side.

Mussel Tacos

An unusual but tasty taco dish.

Preparation time: 30 minutes

Cooking time: 20 minutes

Servings: 2

Ingredients:

2 pounds of mussels

2 tablespoons of butter

1 small-sized onion, sliced

3 garlic cloves, diced

2 teaspoons of ground cumin

2 teaspoons of ground coriander

A pinch of clove

A pinch of cinnamon

Worcestershire Sauce

1/2 cup of freshly squeezed orange juice

1/4 cup of juice from Banana Pepper Jar

15 banana pepper rings

Shredded Cabbage, for slaw

Shredded Carrot, for Slaw

Flour Tortillas

Directions:

1. Mix the shredded carrot and cabbage in a bowl. Season with salt. Combine the orange juice and banana pepper juice in a small bowl and add 1/4 cup of this mixture to the carrot and cabbage mix. Keep aside in the refrigerator.

2. In a skillet, melt the butter and sauté the onions for about 15 minutes until it is browned lightly. Add in the garlic, cumin and coriander and cook for 2 minutes.

3. Add the rest of the half cup of orange/banana juice and scrape the bottom of the skillet in order to deglaze. Add the mussels, cover and leave to simmer for 3-5 minutes. Uncover and check to see if most of the mussels are opened. If not so, cover again and cook for an extra 2 minutes.

4. Begin to remove the opened mussels, ensure that you drain all the juices into the skillet, dispose of the shell, and put the meat into a bowl. Repeat this process for the remaining open mussels and throw away any that remains unopened.

5. Discard the shells and allow the liquid to simmer for about 5 minutes so that it reduces a bit and also cook the acid out. Add the banana peppers and return the mussel meat to the skillet. Allow to simmer for 1 minute.

6. Serve on the tortillas and top with the slaw.

Crawfish Tacos with Avocado Crema

This recipe has all the characteristics of Southern Comfort food.

Preparation time: 15 minutes

Cooking time: 5 minutes

Servings: 6-12

Ingredients:

For the Avocado Crema:

1 cup of sour cream

1 avocado, peeled, pitted and mashed

Juice of 1 lime

Salt

For the Crawfish Tacos:

1 tablespoon of olive oil

1 tablespoon of butter

4 garlic cloves, crushed

1/2 teaspoon of salt

1 teaspoon of cayenne pepper

2 pounds of Louisiana crawfish tails

Juice of 1 lime

1 cup of chopped fresh cilantro

12 taco shells, warmed

Directions:

1. Mix the sour cream, avocado and lime in a medium-sized bowl and with salt.

2. Heat the olive oil and butter over medium high heat in a large pan. Add the garlic, salt, cayenne pepper and crawfish and cook for 2-3 minutes. Add the cilantro and lime juice while stirring.

3. Divide the crawfish mixture between warmed taco shells equally. Top with the avocado crema.

Crab Tacos
Tacos stuffed with a delicious crab mixture.

Preparation time: 30 minutes

Cooking time: 10 minutes

Servings: 8

Ingredients

4 Roma tomatoes, cut into halves, seeded, and chopped

1 large-sized garlic clove, minced

2 large-sized jalapeño chilies, cut into halves, seeded, and chopped, divided

1/2 cup of fresh cilantro leaves, divided

3 tablespoons of fresh lime juice

Kosher salt

Freshly ground black pepper

1 teaspoon of olive oil

1/2 cup of chopped onion

8 ounces of cooked crab, shelled

8 taco shells or tortillas

1 cup of Iceberg lettuce, sliced thinly

1 cup of shredded jack or cheddar cheese

1 avocado, sliced thinly

1/4 cup of chopped green onion

Directions:

1. Preheat the oven to 350F. In a food processor, put the tomatoes, garlic, half of the jalapeño, 1/4 cup of cilantro, and the lime juice and pulse a few times to chop. Add the salt and pepper to season. Keep this aside.

2. Heat oil over medium-heat in a large pan and sauté the onion and rest of the for 4 minutes jalapeño until it is soft. Add the crab to the pan and cook for about 2 minutes just until the crab is warm.

3. Place the taco shells in a baking pan and warm for about 3 minutes in the oven. Set on a platter and spoon the crab mixture evenly among it. Top the crab with lettuce, cheese, and avocado. Sprinkle the tacos with the green onion and left-over 1/4 cup of cilantro.

Jicama Crab Tacos

A delicious combination of crab, mango and avocado.

Preparation time: 15 minutes

Cooking time: 0 minutes

Servings: 8-10

Ingredients:

½ pound of fresh jumbo lump of crabmeat

¼ cup of fresh lime juice

1 teaspoon of lime zest

1 tablespoon of fresh chives, chopped

½ teaspoon of kosher salt

1 large jicama, peeled and thinly sliced

½ cup of mango, chopped

1 avocado, chopped

1 tablespoon of fresh cilantro, chopped

½ cup of Greek yogurt

1 teaspoon of sriracha

1 teaspoon of lime juice

Directions:

1. In a medium bowl, combine the crabmeat, lime juice, lime zest, chives and salt.

2. Put the crab mixture on top of the jicama slices, top with mango, avocado and cilantro.

3. Mix the Greek yogurt, sriracha and lime juice together in a small bowl. Drizzle this mixture on top of the tacos and serve.

RICE/BEANS

Mexican Rice And Beef Tacos

Beef and rice combined in this spicy dish.

Preparation time: 10 minutes

Cooking time: 20 minutes

Servings: 4

Ingredients:

2 tablespoons of spread, divided

1 pound of lean ground beef

1 green bell pepper, diced

1 medium-sized red onion, diced

2 cups of water

1 package of Mexican rice

1 medium-sized tomato, diced

8 taco shells

Directions:

1. Heat a tablespoon of Spread over medium-high heat in a large nonstick pan. Add the ground beef and brown. Add salt and pepper to season, if needed. Remove beef from pan and set aside.

2. Heat the remaining tablespoon of Spread over medium-high heat in the same pan and fry the peppers and onions for about 5 minutes, stirring occasionally, until it is crispy and soft.

3. Add water, rice and tomato while stirring and let it boil over high heat. Turn down the heat and simmer, covered, for 7 minutes or until the rice is soft.

4. Stir in the beef and allow it to be heated well. Fill the taco shells with it and serve topped with your favorite taco toppings.

Taco Rice

This dish can be eaten on its own or served with tacos shells.

Preparation time: 5 minutes

Cooking time: 10 minutes

Servings: 3

Ingredients:

1 (14.5-ounce) can of chicken broth

1 (8-ounce) can of tomato sauce

1 (1-ounce) package of taco seasoning mix

1 1/2 cups of raw instant rice

1 (6-ounce) can of black olives, drained and diced

1 cup of shredded Cheddar cheese

1 cup of sour cream

Directions:

1. Boil the chicken broth, tomato sauce, and taco seasoning in a large pot.

2. Add the rice into the pot while stirring, cover and bring down from the heat. Cover and allow to stand for 5 minutes.

3. Stir in the cheese and olives, combine thoroughly and serve with the sour cream.

Beans And Rice Tacos

You can never go wrong with this classic combination.

Preparation time: 20 minutes

Cooking time: 20 minutes

Servings: 15-20

Ingredients:

2-3 tablespoons of oil

2 cups of cooked brown rice

2 (15-ounce) cans of black beans, undrained

1 cup of picante salsa

1 cup of chopped onion

3-4 chopped cloves of garlic

3-4 fresh jalapeno peppers, diced

1 tablespoon of chili powder

1 tablespoon of ground cumin

20 corn tortillas

Directions:

1. Heat the oil in a large skillet, add the veggies and sauté. Add the rest of the ingredients excluding the tortillas. Bring to a boil and turn down the heat to simmer. Uncover and simmer for 20 minutes or until it is no longer runny.

2. In the meantime, fry the tortillas in oil until it is soft and pliable. Fold and sprinkle lightly with salt.

3. Spoon about 1/4 cup of the bean mixture into the tortillas and top with your favorite toppings.

Vegan Bean and Rice Tacos

A healthy and nutritious alternative to the classic dish.

Preparation time: 12 minutes

Cooking time: 15 minutes

Servings: 4

Ingredients:

12 corn tortilla shells

2 cups of shredded romaine lettuce

1/2 cup of cherry tomatoes, diced

4 green onions, diced

For the bean and rice filling:

2 tablespoons of extra virgin olive oil

1 1/2 cups of prepared brown rice

1 (15-ounce) can of no salt added pinto beans, drained, not rinsed

1 (10-ounce) can of diced tomatoes & green chilies

1/2 cup of reduced-sodium vegetable broth 1/3 cup of frozen corn kernels

1/2 yellow onion, chopped

2 cloves of garlic, minced

2 teaspoons of chili powder

2 teaspoons of cumin

1 teaspoon of sea salt

1/4 teaspoon of black pepper

For the vegan dressing:

1/2 cup of raw unsalted cashews, soaked in water for 2 - 24 hours

3/4 cup of light coconut milk

2 tablespoons of lime juice

2 teaspoons of chili powder

1 teaspoon of cumin

1 teaspoon of onion powder

1 teaspoon of garlic powder

1 teaspoon of agave nectar

1/4 teaspoon of black pepper

1/4 teaspoon of sea salt

A pinch of cayenne pepper

Directions:

1. <u>For Vegan Dressing</u>: Put all the ingredients in a high speed blender and mix for about 2 minutes until it is very smooth.

2. For the Filling: Heat the olive oil in a large skillet over medium-high heat and for about 3 minutes, sauté the onion and garlic until just tender. Add the can of diced tomatoes, pinto beans, spices, salt and pepper. Simmer for about 5 minutes until the juices from the tomatoes are thickened.

3. Add the prepared rice, corn, and veggie broth. Simmer for an extra 5 minutes until the broth is almost completely absorbed. Add salt and pepper to season.

4. To serve, divide the shredded lettuce between the taco shells evenly. Spoon the bean and rice filling on top of the lettuce and garnish with the cherry tomatoes and green onions. Drizzle with the Vegan dressing and serve immediately.

Black Bean Taco

Another vegetarian way to enjoy your favorite taco meal.

Preparation time: 15 minutes

Cooking time: 10 minutes

Servings: 6

Ingredients:

1 tablespoon of olive oil

1 small-sized onion, diced

1 (15-ounce) can of black beans, rinsed and drained

1 (7-ounce) can of green salsa verde

1/2 teaspoon of garlic powder

1/2 teaspoon of chili powder

1/2 teaspoon of ground cumin

6 taco shells

2 ounces of shredded Mexican cheese blend

1 tomato, chopped

1 avocado, sliced

1 cup of shredded lettuce

Directions:

1. Heat the olive oil in a skillet over medium-low heat and sauté the onion for about 5 minutes until it is soft.

2. Add in the black beans, green salsa, garlic powder, chili powder, and cumin while stirring at the same time.

3. Turn down the heat to low and simmer for 5-10 minutes until it becomes thickens.

2. Spoon onto the taco shells and top with the Mexican cheese blend, tomato, avocado, and shredded lettuce.

Sweet Corn and Black Bean Tacos

This dish is fresh, yummy and quite a treat.

Preparation time: 20 minutes

Cooking time: 15 minutes

Servings: 10

Ingredients:

For the corn salad:

2 ears of corn, shucked

¼ cup of chopped cilantro

3 medium-sized red radishes, thinly sliced into small strips

1 teaspoon of lime zest

2 tablespoons of lime juice

1 medium-sized jalapeño pepper, seeded and minced

1 tablespoon of olive oil

¼ teaspoon of sea salt

For the black beans:

2 cans of black beans, rinsed and drained

1 tablespoon of olive oil

1 small-sized yellow or white onion, diced

1 tablespoon of ground cumin

1 cup water

Salt

Black pepper

For the others:

10 small round corn tortillas

1 large-sized avocado, cut into thin strips

Optional garnishes:

Pickled jalapeños

Salsa verde

Directions:

1. For Corn Salad: To prepare the corn salad: Slice the kernels off all four sides of the corn cobs with a chef's knife. Put the kernels in a medium bowl and add the cilantro, radishes, lime zest and juice, jalapeño, olive oil and sea salt. Combine thoroughly. Keep the bowl aside to allow the ingredients marinate.

2. For The Black Beans: Warm the olive oil in a large skillet over medium heat. Add the onions and a dash of salt. Sauté for about 5-8 minutes while stirring occasionally, until the onions are soft and are becoming translucent.

3. Stir in the cumin and cook for about 30 seconds. Add the beans and water. Stir, cover and turn down the heat to allow it simmer for 5 minutes.

4. Remove the lid and mash up at least half of the beans with the back of a fork. Bring down from heat and add salt and pepper to season. Keep covered until it is time to serve.

5. To serve, scoop the black beans down the middle of each of the tortilla and top with the corn salad. Set an avocado slice on the side of the beans and serve with the optional garnishes.

Mixed Bean Tacos

Made with three types of beans and ready in 20 minutes!

Preparation time: 5 minutes

Cooking time: 15 minutes

Servings: 10

Ingredients:

1 tablespoon of olive oil

1/2 red onion, chopped

1 red bell pepper, chopped

1 yellow bell pepper, chopped

1 (15-ounce) can of black beans, rinsed, drained

1 (15-ounce) can of pinto beans, rinsed, drained

1 (15-ounce) can of red kidney beans, rinsed, drained

1/3 cup of chopped cilantro

Juice from 1 lime

2 tablespoons of taco seasoning

Salt

Black pepper

10 Taco Shells

Toppings:

Shredded cheese

Shredded lettuce

Diced tomatoes

Diced avocado

Sour cream

Chopped cilantro

Directions:

1. Heat olive oil over medium-high heat in a large skillet. Sauté the onion and peppers for about 5 minutes until soft.

2. Add the beans, cilantro, lime juice, and taco seasoning while stirring. Cook until it is heated and add salt and pepper to season.

3. Heat the taco shells according to package instructions. Spoon the bean filling on the heated shells and top with your desired toppings.

Mexican Rice And Chicken Tacos

Dinner on weeknights would no longer be boring with this dish.

Preparation time: 20 minutes

Cooking time: 15 minutes

Servings: 8

Ingredients:

1 1/3 cups of cooked long grain rice

8 Taco shells

1 small-sized barbecued chicken, shredded

1 tablespoon of olive oil

1 packet of taco seasoning

4 Green onions, diced

1/4 cup of water

4 Iceberg lettuce leaves, shredded

2 Tomatoes, chopped

3/4 cup of tomato salsa

3/4 cup of sour cream

3/4 cup of Guacamole

Directions:

1. Preheat the oven to 356°F. Place the shells on a baking tray and heat the taco for 5-10 minutes in the oven.

2. Heat oil over medium-high heat in a skillet. Add the taco seasoning and onions, cook for 1-2 minutes until it is tender. Add the water and stir so as to dissolve the seasoning. Add the shredded chicken, cover and cook for 3-5 minutes until the meat is well-heated while shaking the skillet in the process. Add the cooked rice and toss everything to mix.

3. Fill the taco shells with the chicken and rice mixture. Top with the lettuce, tomato, salsa, sour cream and guacamole.

Crockpot Lentil And Brown Rice Tacos

This dish surely tastes as good as it sounds.

Preparation time: 3 minutes

Cooking time: 4 hours

Servings: 15

Ingredients:

1 cup of lentils

½ cup of brown rice

1 onion, chopped

6 garlic cloves, crushed

4 1/2 cups of water

2 tablespoons of chili powder

½ teaspoon of onion powder

¼ teaspoon of red pepper flakes

½ teaspoon of paprika

2 teaspoons of cumin

1½ teaspoons of salt

½ teaspoon of black pepper

Directions:

1. Add all the ingredients to the crockpot and mix together.

2. Cover and cook for 4 hours on high. Stir only once during the last hour of cooking.

Black Bean Tacos With Feta And Cabbage Slaw

Comforting, filling and easy to make.

Preparation time: 3 minutes

Cooking time: 5 minutes

Servings: 4

Ingredients:

1 (15-ounce) can of black beans, drained

1/2 teaspoon of ground cumin

5 teaspoons of olive oil, divided

1 tablespoon of fresh lime juice

2 cups of coleslaw mix

2 green onions, diced

1/3 cup of chopped fresh cilantro

4 white or yellow corn tortillas

1/3 cup of crumbled feta cheese

Hot sauce

Directions:

1. In a small bowl, mash the beans and cumin partially. In a medium bowl, mix 2 teaspoons of olive oil and lime juice, add the coleslaw, green onions, and cilantro and toss to coat. Season with salt and pepper.

2. In large nonstick pan, heat 3 teaspoons of olive oil over medium-high heat. Add the tortillas in a single layer.

3. Spoon 1/4 of the bean mixture on half of each tortilla and cook for 1 minute.

4. Now, fold the tortillas in half. Cook for about 1 minute on each side until golden brown.

5. Fill the tacos with feta and slaw. Serve with the hot sauce.

Steak Tacos And Crockpot Rice
An amazing combination that does justice to your palate.

Preparation time: 10 minutes

Cooking time: 6 hours 10 minutes

Servings: 4-6

Ingredients:

1½ cups of rice

2½ cups of chicken broth

3 garlic cloves, finely chopped

¼ medium onion

2 tablespoons of olive oil

4 tablespoons of finely chopped parsley

1 pound of flank steak

1 smoked chipotle, finely chopped

3 garlic cloves, crushed

Black pepper

1 teaspoon of salt

2 teaspoons of ground cumin

2 teaspoons of oregano

2 tablespoons of olive oil

Pico de Gallo

Flour Tortillas, warmed

Directions:

1. Place the rice, chicken broth, garlic, onion, olive oil, and parsley in a crockpot. Cover and cook for 3-6 hours on high or until the rice is soft.

2. Season the steak with chipotle, garlic, cumin, oregano, olive oil, salt and pepper. Heat a cast iron saucepan over medium heat and cook the steak for 5 minutes per side. Leave the steak to rest for 10 minutes then slice and chop into pieces.

3. Fill the warmed tortillas with the meat and Pico de Gallo. Serve with rice on the side.

VEGETABLE

Summer Veggie Tacos

Prepare this amazing dish with ingredients gotten from your summer garden.

Preparation time: 10 minutes

Cooking time: 15 minutes

Servings: 2

Ingredients:

Olive oil

1 cup zucchini, coarsely chopped

1 clove of garlic, chopped

1/2 medium-sized onion, diced

1/2 fresh jalapeño chili pepper, seeded stemmed and minced

1 large-sized fresh mild green chili, seeded, stemmed, chopped

Salt

A pinch ground cumin

A pinch ground oregano

1 small to medium tomato, diced

4 corn tortillas

4 slices of cheddar cheese

1/4 cup crumbled Mexican cotija cheese

Few sprigs of fresh cilantro, chopped

Directions:

1. In a large skillet, heat 1 tablespoon or two of oil on medium high heat. Add zucchini, garlic, onions, jalapeño and green chilies to the skillet.

2. Sprinkle the veggies with cumin and salt. Stir everything so the vegetables are coated with the oil.

3. Spread the veggies out in the skillet and only stir occasionally, until they are all browned lightly. Add in the chopped tomatoes and oregano while stirring. Reduce the heat to low. Allow to cook for several minutes gently.

4. Warm the tortillas until they are soft and pliable. Fill the tortillas with the veggie mix. Sprinkle the cheese and chopped cilantro. Serve!

Vegetable Tacos With Avocado Tomatillo Salsa
This looks and tastes delicious.

Preparation time: 10 minutes

Cooking time: 30 minutes

Servings: 2-3

Ingredients:

1 small-sized Japanese eggplant, chopped into 1-inch pieces

1 cup of chopped summer squash

1 red bell pepper, deseeded and sliced into 1-inch pieces

1 cup of cherry tomatoes, sliced

Drizzle of extra-virgin olive oil

6 corn or flour tortillas

1 cup of cooked black beans, drained and rinsed

½ avocado, diced

A handful of cilantro

1 serrano pepper, chopped, optional

Sea salt

Freshly ground black pepper

Avocado Tomatillo Sauce:

1/2 cup of tomatillo salsa

¼ cup of pepitas

½ avocado

A handful of spinach

2 tablespoons of olive oil

Squeezes of lime

Sea salt

Freshly ground black pepper

Directions:

1. Preheat oven to 400° F. Line a baking sheet with parchment paper and put the chopped eggplant, squash, red pepper and tomatoes on it.

2. Drizzle with the olive oil and some pinches of salt and pepper to season. Roast for 25-30 minutes until the edges are golden brown.

3. In the meantime, prepare the sauce. Put the tomatillo salsa, pepitas, avocado, spinach, olive oil, lime juice and pinches of salt and pepper in a food processor and blend. Keep chilled until it is time to serve.

4. Serve the tacos with black beans, roasted vegetables, diced avocado, cilantro, serrano pepper, and the avocado tomatillo sauce.

Hearty Eggplant Tacos

A healthy dish loaded with great nutritional benefits.

Preparation time: 10 minutes

Cooking time: 1 hour

Servings: 4-8

Ingredients:

For Vegetable Filling:

1 small-sized eggplant, cut into 1/2-inch cubes

1 1/2 teaspoons of coarse salt

6 tablespoons of olive oil

3/4 cup of chopped onion

2 garlic cloves, finely chopped

1 cup of chopped red bell pepper

1 (28-ounce) can of tomatoes

3/4 pound of plum tomatoes, cut into 1-inch cubes

1 tablespoon of chili powder

1 1/2 teaspoons of cumin

Salt

Pepper

1/4 cup of chopped parsley

1/2 cup of canned dark-red kidney beans, drained

1/2 cup of canned chickpeas, drained

For Tacos:

8 hard corn taco shells

2 cups of finely shredded iceberg lettuce

1 cup of chopped red onion

4 ripe plum tomatoes, chopped

8 ounces of sour cream

8 ounces of grated Cheddar cheese

Directions:

1. Put the eggplant in a colander and sprinkle with salt. Leave to stand for 60 minutes. Use paper towels to pat dry.

2. In the meantime, heat 4 tablespoons of oil in a large pan over medium heat. Add the eggplant and sauté until it is almost soft. Add extra oil if needed. Transfer to a casserole.

3. Heat the rest of the oil over low heat in the same pan and for 10 minutes, sauté the onion, garlic and red pepper. Add to the casserole.

4.Set the casserole over low heat and add the ingredients up through the parsley. Cook for 30 minutes, uncovered while stirring regularly.

5. Add the kidney beans and chickpeas while stirring and cook for 15 minutes. The eggplant skin should be soft. Add more seasoning if required.

6. Spoon 1/4 cup of the veggies in each of the taco shell. Top with some shredded lettuce and a tablespoon each of the onion and tomatoes.

7. Add sour cream dollop, sprinkle with cheese and serve.

Avocado Cream Tacos

A wonderful treat perfect for a lovely day out in the summer.

Preparation time: 15 minutes

Cooking time: 20 minutes

Servings: 6-8

Ingredients:

For Filling:

1 small-sized zucchini, chopped

1 small-sized summer squash, chopped

1/2 medium-sized red onion, chopped

1 ear of sweet corn, removed from cob

1 cup of cherry tomatoes, sliced in half

1 medium-sized red pepper, chopped

2 tablespoons of olive oil

2 garlic cloves, crushed

2 teaspoons of cumin

1/4 teaspoon of salt

For Avocado Cream:

1 ripe avocado

1/3 cup of full fat, plain Greek yogurt

1/4 cup of minced cilantro

1 tablespoon of lime juice

6 to 8 corn tortillas

Feta or goat cheese

Extra cilantro

Directions:

1. Preheat the oven to 400° F. Combine all the vegetables in a bowl and toss with olive oil, minced garlic, salt, and cumin. Roast for 20-25 minutes until they are soft and lightly brown.

2. Meanwhile combine the avocado, Greek yogurt, cilantro, and lime juice either by hand or in a blender.

3. Warm up the tortillas. Fill each shell with the roasted vegetables, avocado cream, a little sprinkle of cheese, and cilantro.

Roasted Veggies And Black Bean Tacos
A nutritious and colorful taco dish.

Preparation time: 15 minutes

Cooking time: 20 minutes

Servings: 9

Ingredients:

3 medium-sized tomatoes, cored and seeded, chopped

2 ears of corn, kernels removed from cob

1 medium-sized zucchini, chopped

1 medium-sized yellow squash, chopped

3/4 small-sized yellow onion, diced

1 red bell pepper, chopped

1 1/2 tablespoons of olive oil

1 1/2 tablespoon of canola oil

1 teaspoon of cumin

1 teaspoon of chili powder, divided

Salt

Freshly ground black pepper

1 cup of canned black beans, drained, rinsed and warmed

1/3 cup of cilantro, chopped

1 1/2 tablespoons of fresh lime juice

Corn or flour tortillas

Queso fresco

Sour cream

Mexican hot sauce

Directions:

1. Preheat the oven to 400 F. Set the tomatoes, corn, zucchini, squash, onion and pepper in a mound on a large baking dish.

2. Mix the olive oil, canola oil, cumin, 1/2 teaspoon of chili powder and salt and pepper in a small bowl. Drizzle the mixture over the vegetables in the baking dish.

3. Toss to coat evenly and spread the veggies into an even layer. Put in the oven and bake for 10 minutes. Now, remove, toss and spread into an even layer as before. Put back in the oven to roast another 10 minutes.

4. Almost at the end of roasting the veggies, toss the black beans with salt and the chili powder that's left.

5. Add this mixture immediately the veggies are done roasting, along with the chopped cilantro. Drizzle lime juice over the top of everything and toss.

6. Serve it warm over the tortillas and top with the Queso Fresco, sour cream and hot sauce, if preferred.

One- Pan Mexican Veggie Tacos
Experience the spicy taste of this one pan dish.

Preparation time: 20 minutes

Cooking time: 30 minutes

Servings: 16

Ingredients:

For Filling:

1 tablespoon of oil

4 carrots, diced

1 potato, diced

2 leeks, diced, optional

1 onion, chopped

1 (15-ounce) can of black beans, rinsed and drained

1 sweet potato, shredded

1 teaspoon of dried oregano

2 tablespoons of ground cumin

A pinch of cayenne pepper

1 teaspoon of chili powder

Salt

Ground black pepper

For Tacos:

16 (6 inch) corn tortillas

1 avocado, peeled, pitted, and mashed

1/2 cup of crumbled queso fresco

1/2 cup of salsa

1/4 cup of finely chopped fresh cilantro

1/2 teaspoon of lime juice

Directions:

1. Heat the oil in a pan over medium heat. Add the carrots and for about 5 minutes, cook and stir until it is lightly browned. Add in the potato and for 5-10 minutes, cook and stir until it is lightly browned and mostly soft.

2. Add the leeks and onion to the pan. Cook and stir for 5-10 minutes until the onion is lightly browned.

3. Mix the black beans, shredded sweet potato, oregano, cumin, cayenne pepper, chili powder, salt, and pepper into the pan and for about 10 minutes, cook and stir until the sweet potato is soft.

4. Bring down the pan from the heat and transfer its contents to a bowl. Use a rubber spatula to scrape the pan clean.

5. Heat each of the tortilla for about 30 seconds on each side in the same pan over medium heat until it is warmed.

6. Spread the mashed avocado on the tortillas and top with the sweet potato mixture, queso fresco, salsa, cilantro, and lime juice.

Slow Cooker Mexican Quinoa Tacos

Incorporate this healthy dish into your life and reap the full benefits.

Preparation time: 5 minutes

Cooking time: 4 hours

Servings: 6-8

Ingredients:

1 cup of quinoa, rinsed

1 cup of vegetable broth

2 (15-ounce each) cans of black beans, drained, rinsed

1 (14.5-ounce) can of diced tomatoes in tomato juice, undrained

1 (10-ounce) can of enchilada sauce

1 (15-ounce) can of corn, drained

3 tablespoons of taco seasoning

Corn or flour tortillas

Optional:

Queso fresco cheese, diced

Avocado

Cilantro

Fresh lime

Directions:

1. Put the quinoa, vegetable broth, black beans, diced tomatoes in tomato juice, enchilada sauce, drained corn, and taco seasoning in a large 6-quart slow cooker. Stir together.

2. Cover and cook for 2 1/2 - 4 hours on high

3. When the quinoa pops and is well-done, serve on the tortillas and top with your preferred toppings.

Soft Vegetarian Tacos

Easy and quite simple to make.

Preparation time: 10 minutes

Cooking time: 10 minutes

Servings: 4

Ingredients:

1-2/3 cups of fresh or frozen corn, thawed

1 small-sized zucchini, finely chopped

1 small-sized onion, finely chopped

1 tablespoon of canola oil

1 (15-ounce) can of black beans, rinsed and drained

1/4 cup of salsa

8 flour tortillas, warmed

1/2 cup of sour cream

1 (4-ounces) cup of shredded cheddar cheese

Directions:

1. Heat the oil in a large pan and add the corn, zucchini and onion. Sauté until it is tender. Add in the beans and salsa. Stir.

2. Cook uncovered for 3-4 minutes over medium heat or until it is well-heated. Stir occasionally.

3. Fill half of each of the tortilla with a heaping 1/3 cupful of the filling and top with the sour cream and cheese. Fold the tortilla over filling, and serve.

Simple Vegetable Tacos

The vegetables in this recipe can be substituted with any other vegetable that is available in your kitchen.

Preparation time: 15 minutes

Cooking time: 8 minutes

Servings: 2

Ingredients:

1½ teaspoon of olive oil, divided

½ yellow onion, diced

½ cup of chopped zucchini

1 cup of sliced mushrooms

½ cup of diced yellow squash

½ jalapeno pepper, seeds & membranes removed, crushed

2 cloves of garlic, crushed

½ teaspoon of oregano

1 teaspoon of ground cumin

1 tomato, diced

¼ - ½ teaspoon of salt

¼ teaspoon of ground pepper

Juice from ½ lime

4 corn tortillas

¼ cup of crumbled cotija cheese

2 tablespoons of minced cilantro

Directions:

1. In a large non-stick pan, heat 1 teaspoon of olive oil over medium heat. Sauté the onions for 2 minutes.

2. Add the remaining ½ teaspoon of olive oil, zucchini, mushrooms, yellow squash, jalapeno, oregano and cumin. Cook for 4-5 minutes until the vegetables are soft.

3. Meanwhile, heat the corn tortillas for about 30 seconds in a single layer on a paper towel in the microwave.

4. Spoon the vegetables on the corn tortillas, and top with the cotija cheese and cilantro.

Vegetarian Taco Salad

This recipe is rich in fiber and really healthy.

Preparation time: 10 minutes

Cooking time: 10 minutes

Servings: 6

Ingredients:

2 tablespoons of extra-virgin olive oil

1 large-sized onion, chopped

1 1/2 cups of fresh or frozen corn kernels, thawed

4 large-sized tomatoes

1 (15-ounce) can of black, kidney or pinto beans, rinsed

1 1/2 cups of long-grain brown rice, cooked

1 tablespoon of chili powder

1 1/2 teaspoons of dried oregano, divided

1/4 teaspoon of salt

1/2 cup of chopped fresh cilantro

1/3 cup of prepared salsa

2 cups of shredded lettuce (iceberg or romaine)

1 cup of shredded pepper Jack cheese

2 1/2 cups of coarsely crumbled tortilla chips

Lime wedges (garnish)

Directions:

1. In a large non-stick pan, heat the oil over medium heat. Cook the onion and corn for about 5 minutes until the onion starts to brown.

2. Chop 1 tomato roughly and add to the pan alongside the beans, rice, chili powder, a teaspoon of oregano and 1/4 teaspoon of salt. Cook for about 5 minutes while regularly until the tomato cooks down. Leave to cool a bit.

3. Chop the other 3 tomatoes and mix in a medium bowl with the cilantro, salsa and the left-over 1/2 teaspoon of oregano.

4. In a large bowl, toss the lettuce with the bean mixture, half of the fresh salsa and 2/3 cup of cheese.

5. Serve this mixture sprinkled with tortilla chips and the left-over cheese. Garnish with the lime wedges and the remaining salsa.

SALSAS / PICKLES / SAUCES

Tomato Salsa

Make this with fresh ingredients.

Preparation time: 6 minutes

Cooking time: 0 minutes

Servings: 3-4

Ingredients:

2-3 medium fresh tomatoes, stemmed

1/2 red onion

2 Serrano chilies or 1 jalapeño chili, stemmed, ribbed, seeded

Juice from 1 lime

1/2 cup of chopped cilantro

Salt

Pepper

A pinch of dried oregano

A pinch of ground cumin

Directions:

1. Coarsely chop the onions, chilies and tomatoes.

2. Put all the ingredients in a food processor and pulse a few times.

3. Put in a serving bowl and season with salt and pepper to taste.

4. Add some more tomato if the salsa is too hot as a result of the chilies. Alternatively, carefully add a few of the chili seeds, or add a little extra ground cumin if it is not hot enough.

5.Leave to sit for an hour so that the flavors can combine.

Simple Tomato Salsa

Serve this with your tortillas and tacos.

Preparation time: 10 minutes

Cooking time: 0 minutes

Servings: 20

Ingredients:

4 large tomatoes, diced

1 onion, chopped

1/2 cup of chopped fresh cilantro

3 garlic cloves, crushed

1 tablespoon of lime juice

1 tomatillo, diced (optional)

Salt

1 jalapeno pepper, crushed

Directions:

1. Combine the tomatoes, onion, cilantro, garlic, lime juice, tomatillo in a medium bowl. Season with salt and mix thoroughly.

2. Add 1/2 of the jalapeno pepper, if you want your salsa to be hotter, add the rest of the jalapeno. Cover and refrigerate until it is time to serve.

Vegetable Pickles

Prepared with some Mexican inspiration.

Preparation time: 25 minutes

Cooking time: 10 minutes

Servings: 10-16

Ingredients:

10 large-sized radishes, sliced thinly

3 large-sized carrots, peeled and sliced thinly

1 pickling cucumber, sliced thinly

1-2 jalapenos, seed and membrane removed, sliced thinly

1 cup of loosely packed cilantro, chopped

3 large cloves of garlic, minced

2 cups of white vinegar

1/2 cup of apple cider vinegar

1/2 cup of red wine vinegar

1 cup of water

1 1/2 cups of white sugar

2 teaspoons of salt

2 (32-ounce) canning jars

Directions:

1. In a bowl combine the vegetables together and toss. Add the cilantro and combine. Keep aside.

2. In a medium skillet, mix together the vinegars, water, garlic, sugar, and salt and bring to a boil. Bring down from heat, and leave the contents of the pan to cool to room temperature. Remove the garlic.

3. Place the vegetables into the jars and pour 2 cups of water into each jar until the vegetables are covered with water.

4. Cover and keep chilled for at least 1 day and up to 4 weeks.

Spicy Tomatoes Salsa

This recipe has been proclaimed by many to be the best.

Preparation time: 20 minutes

Cooking time: 20 minutes

Servings: 56

Ingredients:

8 cups of tomatoes, peeled, diced and drained

2 1/2 cups of onions, chopped

1 1/2 cups of green peppers

1 cup of jalapeno pepper, chopped

6 cloves of garlic, crushed

2 teaspoons of cumin

2 teaspoons of pepper

1/8 cup of canning salt

1/3 cup of sugar

1/3 cup of vinegar

1 (15-ounce) can tomato sauce

1 (12-ounce) can tomato paste

Directions:

1. Combine all the ingredients together and leave to boil slowly for 10 minutes.

2. Seal in jars and cook for 10 more minutes in a hot water bath.

Mexican Salsa

A delicious salsa recipe!

Preparation time: 40 minutes

Cooking time: 20 minutes

Servings: 14

Ingredients:

3 jalapeno peppers

1 medium onion, cut into quarters

1 clove of garlic, cut into halves

2 cans of whole tomatoes, drained

4 fresh cilantro sprigs

1/2 teaspoon of salt

Tortilla chips

Directions:

1. Heat a small cast-iron pan over high heat. Pierce the jalapenos with a small knife and add to the pan. Cook for 15-20 minutes or until the peppers become blistered and blackened. Turn occasionally.

2. Put the jalapenos in a small bowl immediately, cover and leave to stand for 20 minutes. Peel off and dispose of the charred skins, stems and seeds.

3. Put the onion and garlic in a food processor and pulse four times. Add the tomatoes, cilantro, salt and jalapenos. Cover and process until you get the consistency you want. Refrigerate until it is time to serve.

Chunky Salsa
This dish is really hot and spicy!

Preparation time: 45 minutes

Cooking time: 21 minutes

Servings: 56

Ingredients:

5 pounds of tomatoes

5 cups of chopped onions

5 cups of chopped green peppers

2-1/2 cups of chopped sweet red peppers

2 habanero peppers, seeded and chopped finely

1 cup of white vinegar

1 (6 ounces) can of tomato paste

3 teaspoons of salt

Directions:

113

1. Fill a Dutch oven two-thirds with water and boil. At the bottom of each tomato score an "X". Put the tomatoes with a slotted spoon, one at a time, in boiling water for 30-60 seconds. Remove the tomatoes and dip into ice water immediately. Remove and discard the peel and chop the tomatoes.

2. Combine the rest of the ingredients in a stockpot. Add in the tomatoes and stir. Allow to boil over medium-high heat. Turn down the heat, simmer for 15-20 minutes, uncovered, or until you get the desired thickness.

3. Spoon the hot mixture into hot 1-pint jars carefully, leaving about 1/2-inch headspace. Get rid of the air bubbles, wipe the rims and adjust the lids. Process for 15 minutes in a boiling water canner.

Taco Beef Sauce

A wonderful filling for your tacos, tortillas or burritos.

Preparation time: 5 minutes

Cooking time: 25 minutes

Servings: 20

Ingredients:

1 pound of ground beef

1 large onion, chopped

1/2 cup of chopped green pepper

1 clove of garlic, crushed

2 (15-ounce each) cans of tomato sauce

1 tablespoon of chili powder

1/4 teaspoon of pepper

1/4 teaspoon of hot pepper sauce

Directions:

1. Cook the beef, onion, green pepper and garlic in a large skillet over medium heat until the meat is no longer pink.

2. Drain and stir in the rest of the ingredients. Simmer for 15 minutes, uncovered, or until the mixture is thick and bubbling. Stir occasionally.

Jalapeno Dill Pickles
Quick and easy to prepare.

Preparation time: 20 minutes

Cooking time: 0 minutes

Servings: 48

Ingredients:

3 pounds of pickling cucumbers, cut lengthwise into four spears

1/4 cup of snipped fresh dill

1 small onion, cut into halves and sliced

3 cloves of garlic, crushed

1-2 jalapeno peppers, sliced

2-1/2 cups of cider vinegar

2-1/2 cups of water

1/3 cup of canning salt

1/3 cup of sugar

Directions:

1. Mix the cut cucumbers, dill, onion, garlic and jalapenos in a bowl.

2. Mix vinegar, water, salt and sugar in a large skillet. Boil, cook and stir just until the salt and sugar are dissolved.

3. Pour this over the cucumber mixture and leave to cool.

4. Cover tightly and keep chilled for at least 24 hours. Refrigerate for up to 2 months.

Chilled Pickles

Another great way to use up your store of cucumbers and squash.

Preparation time: 25 minutes

Cooking time: 0 minutes

Servings: 24

Ingredients:

3 cups of sliced peeled yellow summer squash

3 cups of sliced peeled cucumbers

2 cups of chopped sweet onions

1 cup of sugar

1-1/2 cups of white vinegar

1/2 teaspoon of salt

1/2 teaspoon of celery seed

1/2 teaspoon of mustard seed

Directions:

1. Put the squash, cucumbers and onions in a large bowl, keep aside.

2. Mix together the rest of the ingredients in a small skillet and bring to a boil. Cook and stir just until the sugar dissolves. Pour this over the cucumber mixture and leave to cool.

3. Tightly cover and keep chilled for at least 24 hours. Use a slotted spoon to serve.

Garden Salsa

For best results, make it with the freshest produce from your garden.

Preparation time: 15 minutes

Cooking time: 0 minutes

Servings: 40

Ingredients:

6 medium-sized tomatoes, finely diced

3/4 cup finely diced green pepper

1/2 cup of finely diced onion

1/2 cup of thinly sliced green onions

6 garlic cloves, crushed

2 teaspoons of cider vinegar

2 teaspoons of lemon juice

2 teaspoons of olive oil

1-2 teaspoons of crushed jalapeno pepper

1-2 teaspoons of ground cumin

1/2 teaspoon of salt

1/4-1/2 teaspoon of cayenne pepper

Directions:

1. Mix all the ingredients in a large bowl. Cover and keep chilled until it is time to serve.

DESSERTS

Ice Cream Tacos

A delicious merger that will leave you wanting more!

Preparation time: 15 minutes

Cooking time: 10 minutes

Servings: 3

Ingredients:

2 tablespoons of cinnamon

1/4 cup of sugar

2 tablespoons of butter

2 cups of chocolate chips

3 small-sized flour tortillas

1/4 cup of rainbow sprinkles

Caramel sauce

Vanilla ice cream

Directions:

1. To prepare the cinnamon sugar: Mix the sugar and cinnamon thoroughly in a small plate.

2. Over a double boiler melt the chocolate chips until they are smooth. Keep aside.

3. Heat the butter in a small skillet over medium heat and sauté the tortillas for 2 minutes on each side until they are crispy and golden. Do one tortillas at a time. Coat both sides of the tortillas with the cinnamon sugar.

4. Fold the tortillas in half and dip its outer edges in the melted chocolate, then dip it in the rainbow sprinkles. Stand the tortillas upright in a muffin

tin that has been turned over. Allow to stand for about 10 minutes so that the chocolate gets hardened.

5. Spoon 3 scoops of vanilla ice cream onto the taco and top with caramel sauce. Freeze for at least 30 minutes until it is hard.

Chocolate Tacos

No one can say no to chocolate!

Preparation time: 20 minutes

Cooking time: 7 minutes

Servings: 4

Ingredients:

1/2 cup of powdered sugar

1/4 cup of all-purpose flour

3 tablespoons of unsweetened cocoa

1 teaspoon of cornstarch

1/4 teaspoon of salt

3 tablespoons of egg whites

1 teaspoon of reduced-fat milk (2%)

1/4 teaspoon of vanilla extract

Cooking spray

1/2 cup of semisweet chocolate chips

1 teaspoon of canola oil

1/2 cup of finely chopped unsalted, dry-roasted peanuts, divided

2 2/3 cups of vanilla low-fat ice cream

Directions:

1. Preheat the oven to 400°F. Mix together the sugar, flour, cocoa, cornstarch and salt in a bowl. Stir in the egg whites, milk, and vanilla into the bowl.

2. Grease a baking sheet with the cooking spray. Draw 4 (5-inch) circles on the baking sheet with your finger. Spoon a tablespoon of the mixed batter onto each of the circle.

3. With the back of a spoon, spread to the edges of the circle and then bake for 6 minutes or until the edges starts to brown. Using a spatula, loosen the edges and remove from the baking sheet.

4. Quickly drape each of the taco over suspended wooden spoons, gently shaping them into a shell. Allow to cool completely. (The shells should be handled carefully as they are quite delicate). Continue this process until the batter has been used up.

5. Mix the chocolate chips and oil in a bowl and microwave for 60 seconds on high or until the chocolate melts. After 30 seconds stir until it is smooth.

6. Gently spread about a teaspoon of the mixture on the top third of the outside of both sides of the now cool shells, and sprinkle about a teaspoon of peanuts on the shell.

7. Fill each shell with a scoop of 1/3 cup of ice cream. Drizzle evenly the rest of the chocolate mixture over the ice cream and sprinkle evenly with the rest of the peanuts.

8. Freeze for 30 minutes at least before serving.

Simple Summer Tacos

Spoil your taste buds with this decadent treat.

Preparation time: 5 minutes

Cooking time: 15 minutes

Servings: 4-10

Ingredients:

For Taco Shells:

1½ cups of flour

¼ cup of sugar

2 eggs and 1 egg yolk

2 tablespoons of butter, melted

2 teaspoons of vegetable oil

1 cup of half & half ⅔

1/2 cup of water

½ teaspoon of vanilla

For Others:

Vanilla ice cream

Whipped cream

Fresh fruit

Caramel sauce or chocolate sauce

Directions:

1. Preheat a non-stick skillet over medium heat and grease with cooking spray. Mix together all the ingredients for the taco shells with a hand mixer until it is very smooth.

2. Pour ¼ cup of the batter onto the skillet and tilt the skillet in a circular motion immediately to allow the batter spread into a larger circle.

3. Cook for about 45-55 seconds, then flip and cook for another 45-55 seconds. Remove to a plate and keep in the fridge to chill. Repeat the process with the rest of the batter.

4. Spoon the vanilla ice cream onto the shells and top with the whipped cream, sliced fruit, and caramel sauce or chocolate sauce. Serve immediately.

Mini Fruit Tacos

Impress your party guests with this mouthwatering appetizer.

Preparation time: 40 minutes

Cooking time: 7 minutes

Servings: 12-15

Ingredients:

For Taco Shells:

24-30 (3 inch) flour tortillas

1 tablespoon of granulated sugar

½ teaspoon of ground cinnamon

Non-stick cooking spray

For Filling:

8 ounces of light cream cheese, softened

1 tablespoon of honey

1 tablespoon of granulated sugar

½ teaspoon of ground cinnamon

½ cup of diced strawberries

½ cup of diced and peeled mandarin orange slices

½ cup of diced pineapple

½ cup of peeled and diced kiwi

½ cup of blueberries

Directions:

1. Preheat the oven to 350F.

2. Combine the cinnamon and sugar in a small bowl. Set the tortillas on a flat surface and spray them with the cooking spray very lightly. Sprinkle the cinnamon sugar evenly over them.

3. Fold each tortilla in half gently and hang them upside down on the rungs of your oven rack. Folding them slightly will give a wider taco shell that is easier to fill. Bake in the oven for 5-7 minutes. Remove and keep aside gently.

4. Whisk the cream cheese, honey, sugar, and cinnamon in a large bowl for about 3 minutes until it is fluffy.

5. Fill each shell with 1-2 teaspoons of the filling and top with the sliced fruits.

Greek Yogurt Banana Pancakes Tacos

You might find it difficult to share this absolutely yummy goodness.

Preparation time: 10 minutes

Cooking time: 10 minutes

Servings: 8

Ingredients:

1/2 cup of oat flour

1/2 teaspoon of baking powder

1/4 teaspoon of salt

1/2 tablespoon of cinnamon, plus extra for topping

1/2 cup of very ripe banana, mashed

1/2 teaspoon of vanilla extract

2 tablespoons of honey

1 large egg

1/4 cup and 2 tablespoons of no-fat vanilla Greek yogurt

1/4 cup of skim milk

1 large banana, sliced

1 cup of no-fat vanilla Greek yogurt

Directions:

1. Grease a large-sized griddle with cooking spray and heat to 350°F.

2. Mix together the oat flour, baking powder, salt and cinnamon in a large bowl and keep aside.

3. Beat the mashed banana, vanilla, honey, egg, Vanilla Greek yogurt and milk in a medium bowl until it is smooth, and there are only a few lumps from the banana. Pour into the oat flour mixture and combine.

4. Using a scant 1/4 cup measurements, drop the batter onto the heated griddle. And with the back of a spoon, quickly spread out the batter thinly. Note that the end result should be thin and look like a tortilla not puffy and big.

5. Cook the pancakes for about 4-5 minutes until they turn golden brown. Flip and cook an extra 4-5 minutes.

6. Spoon about 2 tablespoons of vanilla Greek yogurt, a few slices of banana and a pinch of cinnamon on each pancake.

Cheesecake Tacos

This treat requires no baking at all.

Preparation time: 47 minutes

Cooking time: 25 minutes

Servings: 15-30

Ingredients:

For the Shells:

6 large flour tortillas

Oil

Graham crumbs, optional

For the Filling

8 ounces of cream cheese

1 cup of heavy cream

1 teaspoon of lemon juice

¼ cup of powdered sugar

1 teaspoon of vanilla

For the Topping:

1 can of pie filling, any flavor

Directions:

To make the shells:

1. Cut out circles from the tortillas with a 3.5-inch circle cutter. This should yield about 5 from each of the tortillas.

2. In a skillet, heat about 1 1/2 tablespoons of oil over medium heat. Add the oil with a little scrap of tortilla and ensure that it is nice & bubbling.

3. Put one circle in the oil, with tongs, for about 5 seconds. Turn it over, fold in half and keep it folded for about 5 seconds or until it is browned.

4. Turn it over again and fry the other side until it is crispy. Remove from the oil immediately and give it a little shake.

5. Put it into the graham crumbs if you desire. Keep aside to cool.

To Make The Cheesecake Filling:

6. Mix together the cream cheese and lemon juice until it is soft.

7. Add the whipping cream to the mixture and whisk for 2 minutes on medium.

8. Add in the sugar and beat until it is stiff and fluffy. Put in a ziploc bag and keep chilled for at least 30 minutes.

9. To serve, put the cheesecake filling into each taco circle and top with the pie filling.

Berries Dessert Tacos

Biscuits made with inspiration from tacos.

Preparation time: 30 minutes

Cooking time: 0 minutes

Servings: 8

Ingredients:

2 cups of chopped fresh strawberries

1 cup of fresh blueberries

2/3 cup of sugar

1 cup of whipping cream

1 (16.3-ounce) can of biscuits

2 tablespoons of all-purpose flour

1/4 cup of vegetable oil

Directions:

1. Mix the strawberries, blueberries and 4 tablespoons of sugar in a medium bowl. Cover and keep chilled. Stir occasionally.

2. With an electric mixer, beat the whipping cream in a small bowl on low speed until it is slightly thick. Increase the speed to medium and add 2 tablespoons of sugar to the mixture slowly. Beat until it forms stiff peaks. Cover and keep chilled.

3. Separate the dough into 8 biscuits. Press or roll each biscuit into 6-inch round on a floured surface.

4. Heat 2 tablespoons of oil in a 12-inch pan over medium-high heat. Add 2 of the biscuit to the pan and cook for 30 seconds to 1 minute per side or until they turn light golden brown. Repeat this process with the other

biscuit rounds, adding more oil if necessary. Put on paper towels to drain. Sprinkle a side of the biscuit rounds with the rest of the 4 tablespoons of sugar.

5. Using a slotted spoon, spoon 1/3 cup of the fruit mixture lengthwise in the middle of the biscuit side not coated with sugar.

6. Spoon rounded 1/4 cup of whipped cream along outside the edge of the fruit. Fold the round biscuit over to form a taco.

7. Serve immediately.

Little Taco Desserts
This delightful sweet is perfect for dessert nights!

Preparation time: 20 minutes

Cooking time: 5 minutes

Servings: 12-15

Ingredients:

2 cups of vegetable oil for frying, or more if required

1 (8-ounce) package of cream cheese, softened

1/2 cup of brown sugar

1 teaspoon of vanilla extract

1/2 teaspoon of ground cinnamon

8 large flour tortillas

1/4 cup of cinnamon sugar, or more if required

1/2 cup of sliced green grapes

1/2 cup of crushed fresh strawberries

Directions:

1. In a large skillet or deep-fryer, heat oil to 350F.

2. In a bowl, whisk the cream cheese, brown sugar, vanilla extract, and ground cinnamon together until it is smooth.

3. With a round cookie cutter, cut 3-inch circles out of each of the tortilla. Fold the tortilla rounds into the shape of a taco-shell.

4. Using tongs, hold the folded tortilla and fry for 2-3 minutes in the preheated oil until the taco shape holds and the tortilla turns golden brown. Transfer the tortilla to a plate lined with paper towel. Repeat this process with the remaining tortilla rounds.

5. To serve, sprinkle cinnamon sugar over the cooked tortilla and spread the cream cheese mixture into each shell. Top with grapes and strawberries.

Fruity Tacos
Satiate your sweet tooth with this amazing dessert.

Preparation time: 15 minutes

Cooking time: 0 minutes

Servings: 2

Ingredients:

3 teaspoons of sugar, divided

1/2 teaspoon of ground cinnamon

1/2 cup of cubed fresh pineapple

1/2 cup of chopped, peeled kiwifruit

1/2 cup of chopped fresh strawberries

1 teaspoon of chopped seeded jalapeno pepper, optional

2 (8-inches) whole wheat tortillas, room temperature

Cooking spray, butter-flavored

Directions:

1. In a bowl, combine 2 teaspoons of sugar and cinnamon. Toss fruit with the remaining sugar and jalapeno in another bowl.

2. Coat both sides of the tortillas with the cooking spray. Cook the tortillas for 45-60 seconds on each side in a large pan until it turns golden brown.

3. Remove from the pan and immediately dust with the sugar mixture. Top with the fruit mixture, fold and serve.

Apricot Dessert Tacos
This mouthwatering dessert could turn out to be your favorite.

Preparation time: 20 minutes

Cooking time: 12 minutes

Servings: 8

Ingredients:

1 pound of apricots, peeled and sliced

Juice of 1 lemon

¼ cup of water

1 teaspoon of cinnamon

½ cup of brown sugar

1 cup of mascarpone cheese

¼ cup of powdered sugar

1 tablespoon of vanilla

8 small flour tortillas

2 tablespoons of butter

1 tablespoon of cinnamon sugar

1/4 cup of honey

Directions:

1. Preheat the oven to 425°F. In a large skillet put the apricots and heat over medium heat. Top with the lemon juice and water. Sprinkle the cinnamon and sugar over it. For 10-12 minutes, caramelize.

2. In a large bowl, beat the mascarpone, powdered sugar and vanilla together.

3. Spread the cheese in the middle of each of the tortillas and top with the caramelized apricots.

4. Tightly roll the tortillas and place on a baking dish. Brush with butter and sprinkle lightly with cinnamon sugar.

5. Put in the oven and bake for 12-15 minutes.

6. When it is done, remove. Drizzle with honey immediately and serve.

Fruit Dessert Tacos

This sweet treat is pretty to look at and yum to eat.

Preparation time: 35 minutes

Cooking time: 10 minutes

Servings: 4

Ingredients:

For the tortillas:

3 tablespoons of all-purpose flour

1/4 teaspoon of ground cinnamon

A pinch of salt

1 large egg white

1/4 cup of sugar

1 1/2 teaspoons of butter, melted

1 1/2 teaspoons of canola oil

1/4 teaspoon of vanilla extract

For the fruit salsa

2 tablespoons of sugar

2 tablespoons of lime juice

2 tablespoons of tequila, optional

1 tablespoon of orange liqueur, optional

3/4 cup of chopped pineapple

3/4 cup chopped mango or peach

1 cup chopped strawberries

1 tablespoon of coconut flakes, toasted, optional

Cilantro to garnish

Directions:

1. Preheat the oven to 325°F. Grease 2 baking sheets with cooking spray. Use either parchment paper or foil to line them and coat again.

2. In a small bowl whisk the flour, cinnamon and salt together. In a mixing bowl beat the egg white, 1/4 cup sugar, butter, oil and vanilla until they are smooth. Add the flour-cinnamon mixture and whisk until they blend well.

3. Drop this mixture on the baking sheets by scant tablespoonfuls, let there be 3 cookies on each baking sheet. Spread each mound of batter into a circle 4-4 1/2 inches in diameter using either a metal spatula or the back of a spoon.

4. Bake the cookies one sheet per time for about 7-9 minutes until it is lightly browned. Lift the parchment or foil from the baking sheet immediately and place it on the counter. Loosen the cookies by carefully slipping a flat metal spatula under each cookie.

5. Put back the cookies onto the baking sheet and lay in the oven to soften, for about 1 minute. Remove and drape the cookies over a clean wooden dowel or broom handle that is about 1 inch in diameter. Leave to cool.

6. For the salsa, mix 2 tablespoons sugar, lime juice, tequila and orange liqueur in a medium-sized bowl. Stir so that the sugar gets to dissolve. Add the chopped pineapple, mango and strawberries and gently toss.

7. Just before you serve, fill the tortillas with the fruit salsa and garnish with toasted coconut and cilantro.

OTHERS

Scrambled Egg Tacos

Yes! Tacos can also be made with eggs.

Preparation time: 7 minutes

Cooking time: 3 minutes

Servings: 2-4

Ingredients:

4 large-sized eggs

Kosher salt

Black pepper

1 tablespoon of unsalted butter

4 corn tortillas, warmed

1/2 avocado, sliced thinly

1/4 cup salsa

1 ounce of Monterey Jack cheese, shredded

2 tablespoons fresh cilantro

Directions:

1. Whisk the eggs with ¼ teaspoon each of salt and pepper in a medium-sized bowl.

2. In a large nonstick pan, heat the butter over medium-high heat. Cook the eggs for 2-3 minutes, stirring, until it is set but still soft.

3. Spoon the eggs on the tortillas top with the avocado, salsa, cheese, and cilantro.

Simple Egg Tacos
These tacos are light, easy and delicious!

Preparation time: 10 minutes

Cooking time: 10 minutes

Servings: 2-4

Ingredients:

2 teaspoons of vegetable oil

1/2 small-sized red or green pepper, diced

1/2 jalapeno pepper, seeded and finely chopped

1 garlic clove, minced

2/3 cup of diced ham

1/2 teaspoon of chili powder

4 eggs

1/4 teaspoon of salt

1/4 teaspoon of black pepper

2 teaspoons of butter

4 small whole wheat or regular flour tortillas, warmed

1/2 cup of shredded Cheddar cheese

2 green onions, chopped

For Toppings (optional):

Salsa

Fresh coriander, chopped

Directions:

1. Heat the oil in a medium nonstick pan over medium heat. Add the red and jalapeno peppers and garlic and sauté for 2 minutes or until it is tender.

2. Add the diced ham and chili powder and sauté for 2 minutes or until it is well heated. Transfer to a bowl and cover to keep warm.

3. Beat the eggs, salt and pepper in a small bowl. Melt the butter in the same pan over medium heat. Add the eggs and cook for about 2 minutes while stirring slowly, until it is set but still soft.

4. Fill the tortillas with the eggs top with the ham, cheese and onion. Serve with the toppings if needed.

Salsa Egg Tacos

This dish can be eaten at any time of the day!

Preparation time: 4 minutes

Cooking time: 3 minutes

Servings: 4

Ingredients:

3 large eggs

1/4 teaspoon of salt

1/4 teaspoon of freshly ground pepper

1 cup of grated Monterey Jack or cheddar cheese

1 tablespoon of unsalted butter, melted

3 tablespoons of salsa

4 taco shells

Shredded lettuce

Sour cream

Tomatoes

Optional:

Tortilla chips

Canned black beans

Directions:

1. Beat the eggs in a medium bowl. Add the salt and pepper and 1/4 cup grated cheese to the beaten eggs.

2. Heat a medium non-stick pan over medium-high heat, and melt the butter. Add the egg mixture, and cook for about 30 seconds.

3. Add the salsa to the pan, while stirring the egg mixture slowly to scramble it as it cooks for about 1 minute. Bring down from heat immediately.

4. Spoon the egg mixture onto the taco shells and top with the rest of the cheese, lettuce, sour cream, and tomatoes.

5. If preferred, serve with the tortilla chips or black beans.

Sweet And Spicy Taco

This dish is guaranteed to be a great hit on taco nights.

Preparation time: 10 minutes

Cooking time: 15 minutes

Servings: 10-12

Ingredients:

1 medium red onion, chopped

5 cloves of garlic, minced

2 tablespoons of olive oil

2 pounds of ground turkey

1 pound of ground beef

1 pound of sweet Italian sausage

2 bunches of scallions, only white and green parts, sliced thinly

1 bunch of cilantro, chopped finely

3 tablespoons of ground cumin

1 teaspoon of chili powder

Fine sea salt

1/4 teaspoon of ground pepper

1 tablespoon of Tabasco sauce

1/4 teaspoon of cayenne pepper

1/2 jalapeño pepper, minced

2 1/2 cups of orange juice

1 (4 1/2-ounce) package of corn tortillas, warmed

4 tomatoes, diced

2 heads of romaine lettuce, chopped

2 small-sized onions, chopped

Slices of avocado

1 (12-ounce) package of shredded cheese

1 (16-ounce) carton of sour cream

Directions:

1. Heat the oil in a large pan over medium heat and sauté the onion and garlic for 3-5 minutes, stirring regularly, until the onion turns translucent.

2. Add the ground turkey, beef, and sausage and cook until the meat starts to brown but is not cooked through. Stir with a wooden spoon to break up any large chunks.

3. Add the scallions, half of the cilantro, cumin, chili powder, salt, pepper, Tabasco sauce, cayenne pepper, jalapeño pepper, and orange juice.

4. Cook for about 4 minutes until the liquid has been absorbed, stirring occasionally. Bring down the pan from the heat.

5. Allow everyone make their tacos with the meat, tortillas, tomatoes, lettuce, onions, guacamole, cheese, sour cream, and the remaining cilantro.

Fry Bread Tacos

These are amazing and super worth the hassle!

Preparation time: 30 minutes

Cooking time: 30 minutes

Servings: 4-8

Ingredients:

For Toppings:

1 pound of ground beef

1 (1.25-ounce) package of taco seasoning mix

1 (15.5-ounce) can of pinto beans, undrained

1 cup of shredded Cheddar cheese

2 cups of shredded iceberg lettuce

1/2 cup of picante sauce

For Fry Bread:

2 cups of all-purpose flour

1 tablespoon of baking powder

1 teaspoon of salt

1 cup of milk

4 cups of oil for frying

Directions:

1. In a small skillet, mix the beans and 2 tablespoons of picante sauce over low heat. Cook this combination until it is thoroughly heated.

2. In a large pan on medium-high heat, add the ground beef and taco seasoning mix. Cook, following the instructions on the seasoning mix package. Cover, and keep it warm while you get ready to make the fry bread.

3. Mix together the flour, baking powder, and salt in a medium-sized bowl. Stir in the milk and combine until the dough comes together. Add more flour if needed.

4.Knead the dough for at least 5 minutes on a floured surface until it is smooth. Leave the dough to stand for 5 minutes.

5. Heat the oil in a large and deep saucepan to 365°F. The oil should be about 1 1/2 inches deep. Break off about 3/4 cup sized pieces of dough, and form into round discs shape that is 1/4 inch thick.

6. Make a thinner depressed area in the center of the discs. Fry the dough in the oil until it is golden on both sides. Turn only once. Put on paper towels to drain.

7. Top the fry bread with beans, ground beef, lettuce and cheese. Drizzle picante sauce over it and serve.

Spicy Turkey Tacos

Extremely tasty and finger-licking good.

Preparation time: 10 minutes

Cooking time: 10 minutes

Servings: 4

Ingredients:

3/4- 1 pound of ground turkey breast

8 taco shells

For Seasoning:

4 teaspoons of whole wheat flour

1 teaspoon of chili powder

1 teaspoon of paprika

1 teaspoon of sea salt

3/4 teaspoon of onion flakes

1/2 teaspoon of cumin

1/2-1 teaspoon of cayenne pepper

1/4 teaspoon of garlic powder/

1/4 teaspoon of unbleached cane sugar

1/8 teaspoon of ground oregano

For Toppings:

1/2 cup of reduced-fat sour cream

1/2 cup of 2% cheddar cheese

1/3 cup of picante sauce

2 tomatoes, roughly chopped

1 onion, roughly chopped

1 cup of lettuce, shredded

Directions:

1. In a small bowl, mix together all the seasoning ingredients and keep aside.

2. In a large pan, brown the meat. Add the seasoning mixture and 2/3 cup of water. Combine everything thoroughly. Allow to boil, and then turn down the heat to low. Cook for 10 minutes while stirring occasionally.

3. Heat the taco shells following the package instructions. Spoon the meat onto the taco shells and top with your favorite toppings.

Chili Tacos

This can come in handy when you get tired of the normal taco meat.

Preparation time: 15minutes

Cooking time: 10 minutes

Servings: 4-6

Ingredients:

2 pounds of lean hamburger

2 cans of chili

1 package of corn tortilla

Vegetable oil

Lettuce, shredded

Tomatoes, chopped

Onion, chopped

Cheese, shredded

Sour cream

Picante sauce

Directions:

1. Heat the oil in a pan and brown the hamburger. Add the chili, stir to combine and let it heat well.

2. In a second pan, cover its bottom with enough vegetable oil. Fry the tortillas until they are soft, but slightly stiff around the edges. Put on paper towels to drain.

3. To serve, fill the tortillas with the chili meat and top with the lettuce, tomato, onion, cheese, sour cream and picante sauce.

Spaghetti Tacos

Inspired by the Nickelodeon hit series, i-Carly, this is sure to be a hit with the kids.

Preparation time: 4 minutes

Cooking time: 16 minutes

Servings: 4

Ingredients:

4 ounces of spaghetti

1 teaspoon of olive oil

6 ounces of ground beef

1/2 onion, chopped

1 (14-ounce) can of diced tomatoes

2 teaspoons of chili powder

Kosher salt

Black pepper

8 hard taco shells

Grated Cheddar cheese

Sour cream

Cilantro

Directions:

1. Prepare the spaghetti following the instructions on the package.

2. In the meantime, heat the oil in a large saucepan over medium-high heat. Add the beef and onion. Cook for 5-6 minutes until the meat's color is no longer pink.

3. Add the tomatoes and chili powder. Add ½ teaspoon of salt and pepper. Turn down the heat and allow to simmer for 3-5 minutes until it thickens.

4. Toss with the cooked spaghetti. Spoon onto the taco shells and top with the cheese, sour cream, and cilantro, if needed.

Chili Con Carne Tacos

A delicious piece of Mexican cuisine.

Preparation time: 5 minutes

Cooking time: 47 minutes

Servings: 6-7

Ingredients:

2 tablespoons of sunflower oil

2 onions, peeled and chopped

1 clove of garlic, peeled and minced

1 teaspoon of ground cumin

1 tablespoon of chili powder

1 1/2 pounds of lean minced beef

1 (14-ounce) can of diced tomatoes

1 teaspoon of dried oregano

1 bay leaf

1 tablespoon of tomato puree

1 (14-ounce) can of kidney beans, drained

2-3 ounces of dark chocolate

Salt

Taco shells

Shredded lettuce

Grated cheese

Directions:

1. In a skillet, heat the oil over medium heat and sauté the onion and garlic for about 7-10 minutes or until the onion is tender.

2. Add the cumin and chili to the skillet and cook for 1-2 minutes.

3. Add the beef and cook for about 5 minutes while stirring occasionally, until the meat is browned.

3. Add in the diced tomatoes, oregano, bay leaf and tomato purée. Stir and allow to boil. Turn down the heat and leave to simmer gently for about 30 minutes.

4. Stir in the kidney beans and leave it to get heated. Add the dark chocolate and stir until it melts. Season with salt.

5. To serve, spoon the chili con carne onto a taco shell and top with lettuce and cheese on top.

Crockpot Spicy Taco Potatoes

Another ingenious way of making potatoes.

Preparation time: 5 minutes

Cooking time: 4 hours

Servings: 6-8

Ingredients:

3 pounds of red potatoes, cut into quarters

1 (1-ounce) packet of taco seasoning

2 tablespoons of olive oil

2 tablespoons of salted butter

1 tablespoon of red pepper flakes

Salt

Pepper

Directions:

1. Grease a large crockpot with a non-stick spray.

2. Put all the ingredients in the crockpot and stir to combine.

3. Cover and cook for 3-4 hours on high. If it is possible, stir the mix every hour.

Fried Tacos

This tastes as yummy as it sounds.

Preparation time: 30 minutes

Cooking time: 10 minutes

Servings: 6-12

Ingredients:

1 pound of ground beef

½ cup of chopped onions

½ cup of red or yellow bell peppers, chopped

1 clove of garlic, crushed

1 teaspoon of dried oregano

½ teaspoon of hot smoked paprika

½ teaspoon of ground cumin

¼ teaspoon of dried red pepper flakes

Salt

Pepper

½ cup of tomato paste

4 tablespoons of water

12 tortillas

Canola oil

Sour cream

Salsa

Directions:

1. 1. Brown the beef in a saucepan until it is crumbly. Stir occasionally and break up any large chunks with a wooden spoon. Add the onion, bell pepper and garlic and cook until it is tender while stirring occasionally.

2. Add in the herbs and spices while stirring. Season with salt and pepper. Add in the tomato paste and stir thoroughly to combine. Pour in the quantity of water as desired for consistency. Cover and cook for 10 minutes on low.

3. Spoon a little of the beef mixture on each of the tortillas and roll up. Use a wooden toothpick to secure and fry quickly in a little oil until it turns golden.

4. Serve with the sour cream and salsa.

Crockpot Turkey Taco
A perfect meal for the whole family.

Preparation time: 5 minutes

Cooking time: 5 hours

Servings: 8

Ingredients:

1 pound of lean ground turkey

½ (6-ounce) can of tomato paste

1 small onion, cut into ¼-inch

2 tablespoons of reduced-sodium soy sauce

1 1/2 tablespoons of Mexican- seasoning blend

¼ teaspoon of salt

¼ teaspoon of pepper

Directions:

1. Mix all the ingredients in a crockpot.

2. Cook on low for 4-5 hours.

3. Serve in tortillas and tacos with your preferred toppings.

Slow Cooker Taco Lasagna

The better of two worlds!

Preparation time: 15 minutes

Cooking time: 3 hours

Servings: 8-10

Ingredients:

1 pound of ground beef

1 ounce of package taco seasoning

8 burrito-size flour tortillas

8 ounce of package cream cheese, softened and divided

2-3 cups of shredded Cheddar cheese, divided

1 (15-ounce) can of tomato sauce, divided

Directions:

1. Brown the ground beef in a saucepan over medium-high heat and drain.

2. Add the taco seasoning and cook according to the directions on the packet.

3. Spray the slow cooker with cooking spray lightly. Put two tortilla shells in the slow cooker so that they cover the insert's bottom and come up the sides

4. Spread ¼ cup of the cream cheese over the tortillas and top with ¼ cup of the taco meat, ¼ cup of the cheese and ¼ cup of the tomato sauce. Repeat this process for three more times

5. Cover and cook for 3-5 hours on low.

6. When done, serve with your preferred taco toppings and cheese.

The End

Made in the
USA
Monee, IL